MUSIC THEORY
FOR BEGINNERS

BY R. RYAN ENDRIS

ILLUSTRATED BY JOE LEE

FOR BEGINNERS®

For Beginners LLC
155 Main Street, Suite 211
Danbury, CT 06810 USA
www.forbeginnersbooks.com

A For Beginners® Documentary Comic Book
Copyright © 2015

Cataloging-in-Publication information is available from the Library of Congress.

ISBN # 978-1-939994-46-2 Trade

Manufactured in the United States of America

For Beginners® and Beginners Documentary Comic Books® are published by For Beginners LLC.

First Edition

10 9 8 7 6 5 4 3 2 1

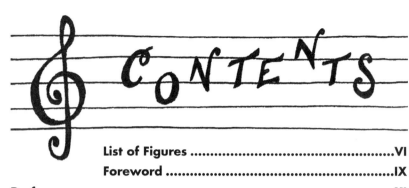

CONTENTS

List of Figures

FOREWORD

MUSIC THEORY FOR BEGINNERS by Ryan Endris fills a need for the serious music lover who wants to go beyond mere listening and seeks to understand the way music is composed and notated. Through lively and well-organized chapters, Endris addresses the rules of melody, harmony, and rhythm that became consolidated in Western European music after 1700 in what is known as the Common Practice. These principles revolve around the implementation of major and minor scales, duple and triple meters, and structures made of a combination of expository musical material, followed by departures or variations and repetitions or recapitulations. Out of these elements the grand structures of Western music have been built, including symphonies, operas, oratorios, concertos, and string quartets.

At the same time, many popular songs that we love for their directness and tunefulness also represent these principles in pristine fashion. Even after the modernist revolutions that surged around the time of World War I, and through the dominance of urban popular dances and song genres from the Americas, the principles of the Common Practice have survived to the present day, forming the core of musical composition. Even when composers use materials outside the Common Practice, they still may reinforce it.

In this work, Professor Endris has taken care to include a brief survey of alternate ways of organizing music, succinctly addressing the emergence of notation in the Middle Ages and experimental scales in the twentieth century, providing a glimpse of how the new has departed from the old and continues to establish itself in opposition to a canonized system.

One of the reasons for the chasm between classical and popular music is the daunting prospect of reading music and analyzing it according to formulas that have the appearance of mathematical equations. The art of reading music is not transferred as commonly as it used to be. Classical music established its high cultural position partly on the edifice of music theory, including the achievement of a notation system that allowed composers to free themselves from the challenges of memorization. This liberation led to ever longer and more complex compositions of art music, performed by ever larger ensembles of virtuoso players and singers, culminating in full symphony orchestras and opera companies. By contrast, popular music has been established on the foundations of folk traditions, ritual practices, and urban social dances that can be learned by ear and played from memory. Today, however, many composers of popular music come to it after mastering the central tenets of Common Practice music theory. Even when they work strictly by ear (which many do not!), the basic rules of music theory still apply.

On some level, then, the dichotomy is false and this book helps in breaking it down. There remains something very impressive about classical musicians who learn to read music and master their instruments from a very young age, but in a parallel fashion, music can be enjoyed even more by listeners who are able to follow the score. Once you recognize the different tonal areas and their behaviors through a piece—the scales and the rhythms, the expositions, the developments, and the recapitulations—new landscapes of meaning and understanding open up. The events of history, the stylistic trends of individual artists, and the preoccupations of every age are displayed before us by means of a new associative power and deeper insight.

Music Theory For Beginners is a wonderful key to music theory and potentially an excellent companion to any book on music history. It will open the doors to music reading and inspire the reader to new curiosities and new adventures in this great art, in all its forms.

—Carmen-Helena Téllez

Professor of Conducting and Director of the Interdisciplinary Sacred Music Drama Project at the University of Notre Dame. A composer and interdisciplinary artist as well as a scholar, she has commissioned and premiered many new works and has led performances representing virtually all genres and periods around the world. She has been called "a quiet force behind contemporary music in the United States today."

PREFACE

MUSIC THEORY IS the study of how music is written and the fundamental elements of music in the modern Western music tradition, known as the Common Practice (ca. 1700–1917). *Music Theory For Beginners* was developed for anyone interested in learning to read and write music, a task that can be quite daunting for novices. This text will allay any such fears and set you on the path to learning what all those dots, lines, and symbols actually mean. It provides the necessary scholarly muscle to entice and inform the reader, yet it does not require any prior knowledge of music or force the reader to wade through hundreds of pages of jargon and details. Anyone can pick up this book and instantly start learning about—and understanding—music theory. Some terminology may already be familiar to you, even if you have no prior musical knowledge; most of it, however, likely will be new. In any case, a straightforward explanation of music theory terminology is provided in both the main text and the glossary. The words are both italicized and bolded the first time they are presented, to draw the reader's attention.

Learning to read and write music is very similar to learning a new language. You might find it helpful to read a section once, let it digest, and then review it again at a later time. Whether your goal is to gain a cursory understanding of music, become fluent in reading music, or start composing music of your own, this text will provide everything you need to know for a solid foundation in music theory. While many music theory textbooks provide elaborate examples and figures from the classical repertoire, this book does not. This text presents musical figures in a simple, straightforward fashion to help readers easily understand the concepts. Examples, background information, and sidebar material are drawn from popular as well as classical music. (Not covered in this book is guitar notation, or tablature, since it is frequently taught in jazz methods books.) I strongly encourage you, however, to follow up your studies here by reading *The History of Classical Music For Beginners* and listening to classical music of your own choosing. I think you will find that it only enhances your experience of *Music Theory For Beginners*!

—R. Ryan Endris
Hamilton, New York
January 2015

AS WE STUDY how music is put together, we will examine the four main characteristics of musical sound: pitch, duration, volume, and (to a lesser extent) timbre. **Pitch** is the result of the movement of air molecules caused by vibration, and we describe it in terms of highness and lowness. Higher pitches have higher frequencies, or vibrations per second. (Scientists measure frequency in hertz.) Lower pitches have lower frequencies. For example, the subwoofer in a home theater system produces all the low sounds in a movie (low-frequency pitches), while a dog whistle produces such high-frequency pitches that they are undetectable by the human ear. **Duration** is exactly what you would think it would indicate: the length of time that a sound lasts. It consists of the initial attack, or onset of the sound, and the amount of time the sound is sustained.

THAT'S QUITE A DURATION.

One of the key characteristics of musical sound is volume, otherwise known as the **dynamic level**. While scientists indicate specific measures of loudness and softness in terms of decibels, musicians use less precise (and sometimes subjective) Italian terms like *forte* ("loud"), *piano* ("soft"), *mezzo-forte* ("medium-loud"),

and *pianissimo* ("very soft"). Based on these, you can probably figure out that the terms for "very loud" and "medium soft" are *fortissimo* and *mezzo-piano*, respectively. The fourth characteristic, **timbre**, is more difficult to define. Musicians often refer to it as the "color" of a particular sound. For example, almost anyone — even non-musicians — can distinguish between the sound of a guitar versus the sound of a flute versus the sound of a violin, even if they are playing the exact same pitch. The distinguishing characteristic in the quality of sound that each one makes is timbre.

We also examine music with regard to six key elements: rhythm, form, melody, harmony, timbre, and texture. We can think of these as pairs that work together on a micro and macro level. Rhythm, as you will read in Chapter 1, comes from the steady pulse of the music, while form describes the unfolding of the musical work as a whole. Just as a play or novel may take its form from a sequence of rising action, climax, and falling action, musical works, too, have both small- and large-scale structures. Melody is the linear unfolding of pitch over time, while harmony is the simultaneous sounding of multiple pitches in a particular instance. Finally, timbre is the quality or color of an instrument, voice, or any combination of them, whereas texture is determined by the number of such instruments or voices playing at a given moment.

While we will spend more time learning about some of these elements (melody and harmony) than others (timbre and texture), it is important to understand that all of these characteristics and elements comprise what we call music.

I.

NO PITCHES ALLOWED—RHYTHM, BEAT, TEMPO, AND METER

Chapter 1:

THE BUILDING BLOCKS OF RHYTHM

RHYTHM, BEAT, TEMPO: these are words we use all the time, often in reference to classical music, but also in talking about popular music and even the way people speak. You might hear someone casually say, "She has really good rhythm," or "I really like the beat of that song." Perhaps you've heard a political analyst comment on the rhythm or tempo of a presidential speech. We've all heard these terms, but what do they actually mean? These three words—rhythm, beat, and tempo—are often used interchangeably and *incorrectly*. They are never, ever the same thing, and your task for this chapter is to learn what differentiates them and how they are related.

Without even knowing it, you're most likely familiar with beat. Have you ever caught yourself tapping your foot or clapping along with a song? What you're mostly likely tapping—or clapping—out is the beat. **Beat** is the underlying pulse in music. It is steady like a heartbeat (unless there's an arrhythmia!), and it is ever-present, even during silences.

LADE DADE DA.
LADE DA DE DE.
THE BEAT GOES ON...

CHER

Not everyone is a fan of electronic dance music, but if you've ever been to a dance club or just listened to electronic dance music, then you *definitely* know what **beat** is. That continuous "thud-thud-thud-thud" that rings in your ears and pounds in your chest is the beat of the music.

Tempo, the Italian word for *time*, is the speed of the beat. You can also think of tempo as a way of describing how fast or slow the music is played. One usually thinks of a funeral march as having a slow tempo, while a marching band in an Independence Day parade typically plays music with a fast tempo.

Classical music usually, but not always, uses Italian words to describe various *tempi* (the plural of *tempo*). For example, *allegro*, meaning *happy*, describes a faster tempo; *largo*, meaning *broad*, describes a slower tempo. Sometimes composers leave the tempo of their composition up to the performer with a simple marking of *allegro* or *lento* (slow). Others, however, are *very* specific. At the beginning of his *Mass in C*, for example, Beethoven indicates the tempo as *Andante con moto assai vivace quasi allegretto ma non troppo* ("A walking pace with motion, always lively, somewhat a bit on the fast side, but not too much"). While seemingly very specific (at least in Beethoven's mind), his instructions have remained quite ambiguous for those left to interpret them!

Of our first three essential terms, the final one you'll need to understand is rhythm. **Rhythm** is the pattern of sound and silence in music; more simply, think of it as the way the words go in a song. When you're tapping your foot to a song, that's the beat; but when you're singing, saying, speaking, or whispering the words to the song, you're singing, saying, speaking, or whispering the rhythm. Singing along with your favorite guitar solo in the middle of the song? You're singing the rhythm. But what about when there's silence in the middle of a song? Remember that silence, too—not just the sound—is part of the rhythm. And of course, the beat goes on, even when there is silence in the rhythm. Rhythm can also be thought of as the general motion of music, with beat as its fundamental unit (more on this in Chapter 2).

One of the key elements of rhythm is duration. Is a particular sound made for a long time (like sticking your tongue out and saying "ah" as the doctor examines your throat), or is the sound quick and short, like when someone yells, "Ouch!"? You can think of rhythmic values very much like measuring cups that hold different (and related) amounts of dry or liquid foods. For example, one cup is equivalent to two ½ cups, which is an aural perception; each ½ cup contains two ¼ cups, and each ¼ cup is made up of 4 tablespoons. Rhythmic values essentially tell us the quantity or duration of sound; they have nothing to do with the dynamics of the sound (loudness or softness).

Figures 1.1 and 1.2 identify the most common rhythmic values and their relationships to each other. Frequently in modern musical piece, the longest note value is a whole note, which in Figures 1.1 and 1.2 receives four pulses. The half note receives two pulses, and the quarter note receives one pulse. Believe it or not, there is such a thing as less than a full pulse! An eighth note receives half a pulse, and a sixteenth note receives a quarter of a pulse. The rhythmic values continue to divide beyond this point (infinitely), but rhythmic values shorter than a sixteenth note are not commonly found in most music. Of course, because duration applies to both sound and silence, the latter are represented by corresponding symbols called **rests;** likewise, they can take the form of a whole rest, half rest, and so on. While the whole rest and half rest may look identical, their placement on the staff (the five parallel lines used to "hold" the notes and rests) determines their value: a whole rest "hangs" from the third line, while the half rest "sits" on it.

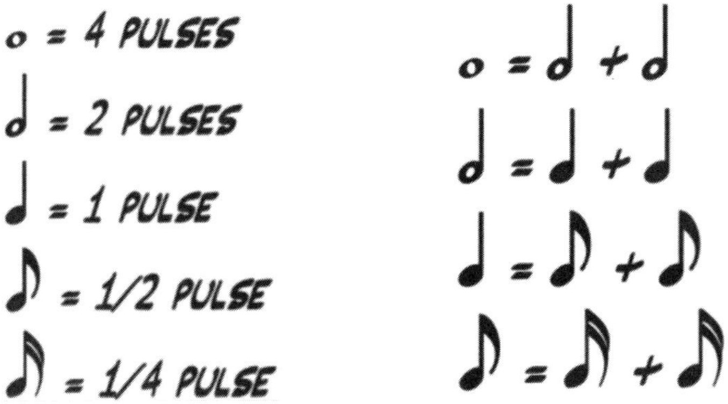

o = 4 PULSES   o = ♩ + ♩

♩ = 2 PULSES   ♩ = ♩ + ♩

♩ = 1 PULSE   ♩ = ♪ + ♪

♪ = 1/2 PULSE   ♪ = ♪ + ♪

♪ = 1/4 PULSE   ♪ = ♪ + ♪

Figure 1.1. *Rhythmic values of sound as represented in musical notation*

— = 4 PULSES

— = 2 PULSES

𝄽 = 1 PULSE

𝄾 = 1/2 PULSE

𝄿 = 1/4 PULSE

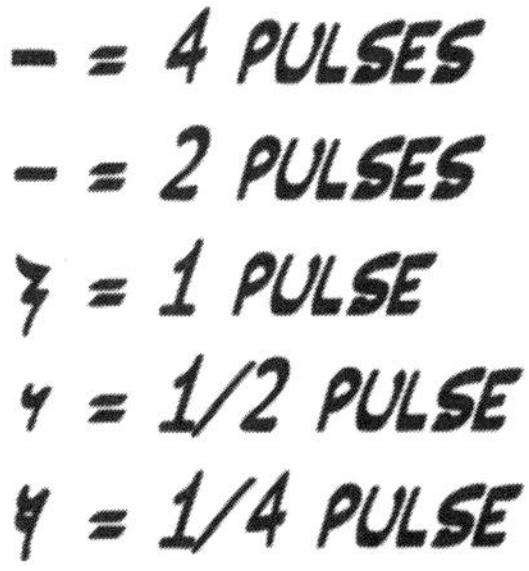

Figure 1.2. *Rhythmic values of silence (rests) as represented in musical notation*

Up to this point, we've discussed beat, tempo, and rhythm, and we've learned the various durations of rhythms in music. These rhythms, of course, are all relative to meter, the framework that brings all of these elements together. We'll learn about that in the next chapter.

Chapter 2:
METER, THE FRAMEWORK FOR RHYTHM

THIS MIGHT BE the perfect time for you to grab one of your favorite tunes and listen to it while tapping your foot along with the beat. You probably notice that some beats feel stronger, while other beats feel weaker. This combination of strong and weak beats in a recurring pattern is what we call *meter*.[1] Modern music, generally, follows some very specific patterns, or meters. And of course, meter is directly related to the rhythmic values we learned about in the previous chapter. Meters are divided into two categories: simple meter and compound meter.

Beats typically divide into either two or three parts. *Simple meters* are meters with beats that divide into two, while *compound meters* have a beat that divides into three. For example, a meter that uses the quarter note as the beat would divide into two eighth notes. Take a look at Figure 2.1, an example of simple meter. As you'll see, each quarter note divides into two eighth notes in each measure. You'll also notice that there is an accent mark (>) above the first note in each group. This reminds you that the first beat in *any* meter is always the strongest!

1. In earlier Western chant music and in contemporary artistic pieces, the strong/weak scheme is non-existent or intentionally avoided. The concept of strong beat versus weak beat derives from dance music and the organizational power of the body moving to music, i.e., dance.

Figure 2.1. *Simple meter demonstrating a division of two eighth notes per quarter note*

In Figure 2.1, the quarter note receives the beat and divides into eighth notes. But what if a different note value receives one beat, such as a whole note or a half note or even an eighth note? It will still divide into two beats of half the value of the principle beat, as demonstrated in Figure 2.2.

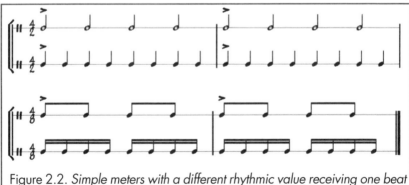

Figure 2.2. *Simple meters with a different rhythmic value receiving one beat*

You probably also noticed a couple of other things about these examples. One is that the rhythms are grouped together and separated by lines. The lines are called **bar lines**, and they delineate a **measure**. A measure is simply a grouping of notes with a meter (remember—a meter is a specific combination of strong and weak beats that repeats over and over again), and the bar line is used to show where each measure starts and ends. Even if there were no bar lines (they didn't even exist in the fifteenth century!), the music could still be played; measures just make it easier for musicians to keep track of where they are in the music.

The other important symbol that you may have noticed is a set of numbers at the start of each line. These two numbers, indicating the time signature, give musicians valuable information about the meter. The *time signature* represents the meter with two numbers: the top number indicates how many beats there are in each measure; the bottom number indicates which rhythmic duration (e.g., quarter note, half note) receives one beat or pulse. The top number can range anywhere from 1 to infinity, but the bottom number must correspond to a specific rhythmic value. The most common bottom numbers are 2 for a half note, 4 for a quarter note, and 8 for an eighth note, but 1, 16, 32, 64, and so on are possible as well. Why can't the bottom note be a 7 or 9? Because there is no such thing as a seventh note or a ninth note (refer back to Chapter 1).

The top number generally gives three options for the type of simple meter: duple meter (2 beats per measure); triple meter (3 beats per measure); or quadruple meter (4 beats per measure). Of course, a meter could have 5 beats per measure or 7 beats per measure, but these are irregular and not commonly encountered. Whether the meter is simple duple, simple triple, or simple quadruple, the important thing to remember is that the beat always subdivides into two (see Figure 2.3). Examples include "Oh! Susannah!" for simple duple meter, "The Star-Spangled Banner" for simple triple meter, and "Joyful, Joyful, We Adore Thee" (Beethoven's "Ode to Joy") for simple quadruple meter.

"Ode to Joy" comes from the final movement of Beethoven's Symphony No. 9, also known as "the Choral Symphony." This work is iconic not only for its unprecedented length, but also for its inclusion of voices as part of the orchestral texture. For lyrics, Beethoven began with a poem by Friedrich Schiller and added text of his own. At the time of the symphony's composition and premiere in 1824, Beethoven had fallen profoundly deaf; sadly, he insisted on "directing" the performance himself. The theater's music director had to instruct the performers to ignore Beethoven's directions, as he was conducting music that he could not actually hear.

Since its composition, "Ode to Joy" has become a permanent fixture in Western culture. It served as the national anthem for the Republic of Rhodesia (now Zimbabwe), albeit with different words, and an instrumental-only adaptation is the official anthem of the European Union today. If you're a churchgoer (or have seen the movie Sister Act), you'll likely recognize the tune as "Joyful, Joyful, We Adore Thee."

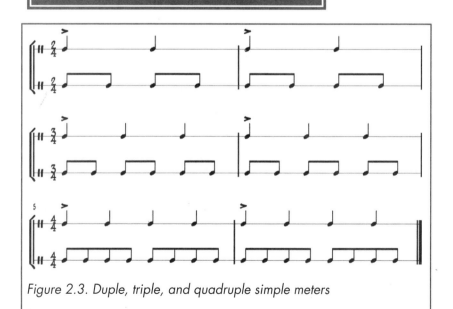

Figure 2.3. Duple, triple, and quadruple simple meters

The other type of meter is called compound meter. Compound meters can be duple, triple, or quadruple just like simple meters; however, the beat divides into *three* parts instead of two. Because of this, the rhythmic value that receives one beat cannot simply be a quarter note or any other note; in order to be divided into three, it must be half again as long in duration. How does one make the note half again as long? It's a simple as adding a dot after the note.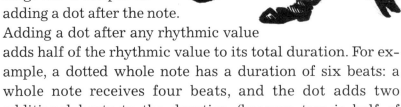

Adding a dot after any rhythmic value adds half of the rhythmic value to its total duration. For example, a dotted whole note has a duration of six beats: a whole note receives four beats, and the dot adds two additional beats to the duration (because two is half of four). Congruently, a dotted quarter note has a rhythmic value of one-and-a-half beats. Figure 2.4 shows how these dotted rhythmic values translate to duple, triple, and quadruple compound meters.

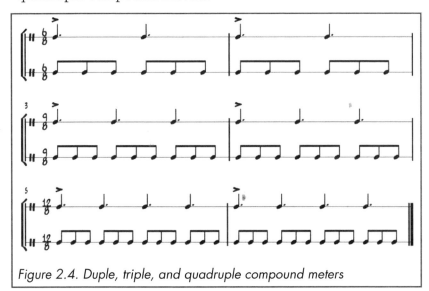

Figure 2.4. Duple, triple, and quadruple compound meters

You have probably noticed that the top number of the time signatures in Figure 2.4 is not a 2, 3, or 4, as in simple meters. This might be a bit confusing, since the numbers are 6, 9, and 12. Simply put, we have no other way to indicate in modern notation that the beat is divided into three while still using a 2, 3, or 4 as the top number. Instead, we count the total number of eighth notes and use that as the top number; however, there are *not* 6, 9, or 12 beats in each measure. There are 2, 3, and 4 beats in each measure of duple, triple, and quadruple compound meter, respectively.

In the late twentieth-century, music began to be seen as spatial, with masses of sound moving through space and interacting with each other. This modernist idea is rooted in measuring musical time not with beats and meter, but with seconds of time. The concept of sound masses moving through space is best exemplified in the compositions of György Ligeti (1923–2006), whose music—by no coincidence—was made famous in the science fiction film 2001: A Space Odyssey. The soundtrack for the movie also highlighted the music of other "classical" composers, bringing old music into modern popular culture. Aside from the music of Ligeti, Stanley Kubrick's film featured the music of Richard Strauss, as well as Johann Strauss, Jr.'s Blue Danube Waltz, which may be the most recognizable waltz of all time. And no, Richard and Johann are not related!

The one thing that all these different meters have in common is that they deal with rhythms that occur *on* the beat. However, as you'll notice when singing along with your favorite songs, some of the words occur between the beats. First, let's identify what's happening. When rhythms in between beats are accented, that's called *syncopation*. And because things no longer line up neatly with the beat, some notes have to be tied together. A *tie* is a curved line

that connects two notes of the same pitch and essentially unites them into a single duration equal to their two separate durations. Thus, a quarter note tied to another quarter note equals two beats, the same as a half note. Figure 2.5 demonstrates an example of syncopation in the top line against the quarter note beat in the bottom line.

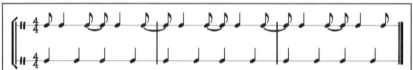

Figure 2.5. The use of ties to create syncopation (top line) against a quarter note beat (bottom line)

"It Don't Mean a Thing (If It Ain't Got That Swing)!"

That's the title of a popular song, now considered a standard in the jazz repertoire, by the legendary Duke Ellington (1899–1974). The song has been covered by some of the world's most famous musicians, from Louis Armstrong, to Ella Fitzgerald, to Tony Bennett. Syncopation is one of the most identifiable characteristics of jazz. (Keep singing the song and you'll notice that all of those "doo-wahs" are syncopated). The beat in jazz music is always clear and strong, but the rhythms often are placed before or after the beat, helping to give it that "swing."

The last thing you need to know about rhythm before we bring this chapter to a close is how to count or say the different kinds. In simple meters, the beat is divided into its number followed by the word *and*. So, for example, a quadruple simple meter would be counted as "ONE and TWO and THREE and FOUR and." In simple meters, the beat is divided into its number followed by "*and a*." For example, a triple compound meter would be counted as "ONE and a TWO and a THREE and a FOUR and a." While all of this might seem a bit complex or overwhelming, it will become second nature to you with time and practice. Now go grab a piece of music and start practicing those rhythms!

II.

MUSICAL NOTATION

Chapter 3

NOTATING PITCH (AND WHAT PITCH IS)

NOW THAT WE have learned how to write rhythms on a single line, we turn to the question of how to notate the highness or lowness of pitch. Logically enough, a system was developed to indicate pitch vertically on a staff. A *staff* (pl. *staves*) consists of five parallel lines that are separated by four spaces. The lines are numbered one through five from the bottom to top, and the spaces are numbered one through four, again from the bottom to top. Figure 3.1 shows an example of a staff.

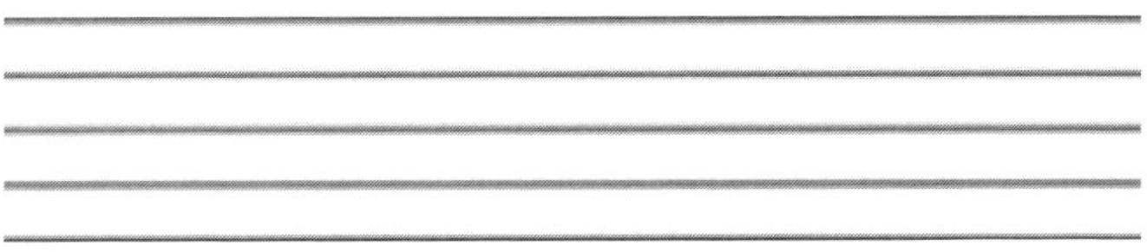

Figure 3.1. *Empty staff*

Noteheads are marked on the staff to indicate highness and lowness of pitch. **Noteheads** are the small oval shapes used to notate pitch. Higher pitches are placed higher on the staff; lower pitches are placed lower on the staff.

In Figure 3.2, the second note (on the third space) is higher than the first note (on the third line). Even a person who does not read music can logically deduce that a note that is higher on a vertical plane has a higher pitch than a note lower on the plane. Eventually we will add stems (the vertical lines coming from the noteheads) and sometimes flags (the small banners that hang from the stems of eighth notes and notes of shorter duration) to indicate rhythm. But for now, let's focus exclusively on pitch.

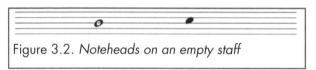

Figure 3.2. *Noteheads on an empty staff*

Before we continue with notating pitch on the staff, however, it is important to understand that each note in music has a letter name—A, B, C, D, E, F, or G. This letter name is determined by the note's position on the staff in conjunction with the clef being used (more on clefs in a bit). So what do you do when you are counting pitches upward and you run out of letters beyond G? You simply start over again with A. The same applies below A; you simply continue backwards with G, followed by F, E, etc. If we consider this pattern of seven pitches, we notice that every eighth letter is the same. We say that these pitches are an **octave** apart. The range from one A to the A above or below is an octave.

Although the letter names apply to notes played on any Western instrument, the piano keyboard is our best friend in teaching music theory. On the piano keyboard, the white keys follow the same A-G pattern of letter names and repeat it in each direction to the end of the keyboard. Most pianos have 88 keys; electronic keyboards usually have fewer, sometimes as few as 61. Figure 3.3 will help you identify pitch location on the keyboard. The white key immediately to the left of any group of two black keys is always a C; the white key immediately to the left of any group of three black keys is always F.

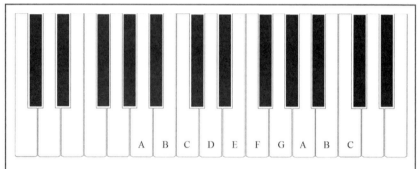

Figure 3.3. *Piano keyboard and letter names*

The black keys in between the white keys are exactly what you might think they are: pitches in between the white keys. For example, the black key between A and B in Figure 3.3 is equidistant from them and identified through the use of accidentals. **Accidentals** are symbols used to identify pitches as higher or lower than what was previously indicated. The three accidentals are **sharp (#)**, to raise the pitch one half-step; **flat** (b), to lower the pitch one half-step; and **natural (§)**, which cancels a sharp or flat. Thus, in the example of the black key between A and B, we can identify it as either A-sharp or B-flat, depending on its context in the music. We call these pitches **enharmonic equivalents**—two pitches that are spelled differently but sound exactly the same.

The piano is perhaps the most recognizable musical instrument in the world, and it is ubiquitous: you can find them in bars, hotels, department stores, homes, and schools, among many other places. The piano is even a common subject for popular songs, such as "Piano Man" by Billy Joel and "I Love a Piano" by Irving Berlin, the guy who also wrote "Blue Skies" and "White Christmas." But how did the piano come into existence? Before the piano, starting in the Renaissance era, the harpsichord was the keyboard instrument of choice.

Harpsichords are easily identified by the inversion of key colors compared to the modern piano. (The white keys on a piano are black on a harpsichord, and the black keys on a piano are white on a harpsichord). How a harpsichord produces sound can also be understood as an "inversion" of the piano's mechanisms. When one presses a key on a harpsichord, a small quill called a "plectra" plucks the string; when one presses a key on a piano, a small hammer strikes the string (which is why the piano is considered a percussion instrument). With the harpsichord there is no variation in dynamic; the string is either plucked or it isn't. But the piano was a huge step forward in music technology, because it allowed variations in dynamics and touch, depending on how a key is struck.

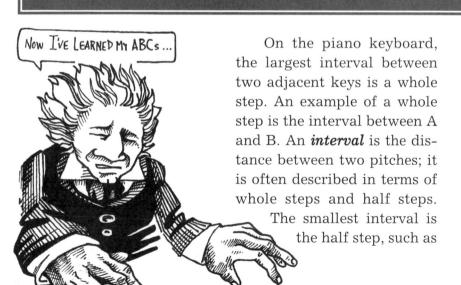

Now I've Learned My ABCs...

On the piano keyboard, the largest interval between two adjacent keys is a whole step. An example of a whole step is the interval between A and B. An *interval* is the distance between two pitches; it is often described in terms of whole steps and half steps.

The smallest interval is the half step, such as

Modernist composers, however, just couldn't leave well enough alone, finding ways to create new sounds (timbres) on the piano. American composer John Cage (1912–1992) paved the way for the "prepared piano," in which everyday objects like bolts, nuts, screws, and rubber were placed on or in between the piano strings. Henry Cowell (1897–1985) didn't go quite as far as Cage, but he did compose music that asked the performer to reach inside the piano and pluck, scrape, or tap on the strings in lieu of playing the keys on the keyboard.

the interval between A and the black key on either side of the A. Although whole steps are usually found between adjacent letter names, there are exceptions (between B and C and between E and F). You'll notice that there is no black key between these sets of keys. It's important to remember also that a whole step is comprised of two half steps.

In music we say "A-sharp," but in musical notation we always place the accidental before the notated pitch—the musician needs to know the pitch is altered before he is about to play it; afterwards would be too late!

To identify pitches on the staff, we need a symbol to tell us what pitches the lines and spaces represent; the staff in and of itself does not provide this information. The symbol used to identify the pitches of the lines and spaces is called a *clef*. Generally, two different clefs are used. The *treble clef,* also called the G clef, is used to identify the second line (from the bottom) as the pitch G. It is commonly used for higher instruments and voices, or for playing the right hand part in piano music. The *bass clef,* also called the F clef, is used to identify the fourth line as the pitch F. It is commonly used for lower-sounding instruments and voices, or for playing the left hand part of piano music. Figure 3.4 shows a *grand staff*, or two staves connected by a brace, with the top staff having a treble clef and the bottom staff having a bass clef. The grand staff is used primarily in piano music, although it is also used for choral music or any other type of music where the range of pitches is too wide for a single staff.

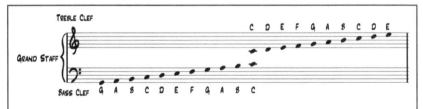

Figure 3.4. *Grand staff with treble clef on top staff and bass clef on bottom staff*

Figure 3.4 also illustrates two other important concepts. The first is that the C in the middle (the one that seems to be floating in between the staves), is the exact same pitch on each staff, represented differently in the two clefs. This particular C is known as "middle C"; it is found in the middle of any piano keyboard. The second important concept is that of ledger lines. **Ledger lines** are the little lines added below or above a staff to extend its range. Theoretically, ledger lines extend infinitely in either direction of the staff. The highest-sounding instruments, such as violins and flutes, often need multiple ledger lines above the treble staff. The lowest-sounding instruments, such as the tuba and string bass, often need multiple ledger lines below the bass staff. The ledger lines are the same distance apart as the lines on the staff, and they do not connect to each other in any way.

Chapter 4:

THE EVOLUTION OF MUSICAL NOTATION

NOW THAT YOU have an understanding of the basic elements of modern music notation, it is appropriate (and important!) to understand how we arrived at the notation system used today. We take for granted the fact that printed music is easily and readily available. Today you can even buy and print music in the comfort of your own home. But how was music communicated 2,000 years ago? Or even 500 years ago? We actually know very little about the music of antiquity, but the pieces of history that do remain clue us into a few important facts about ancient music. The music of the ancient world placed particular emphasis on the relationship between rhythm and text, and melody was an important element. We also know that there was no codified system for dictating music. Without one, music was generally transmitted orally, relying on the memories of musicians to pass from generation to generation.

Let's travel back two and a half millennia to ancient Greece, circa 500 B.C.E. For the ancient Greeks, music was not only an art, but also a science. Students studied music along with mathematics and astronomy; numbers therefore played a large role. Philosopher and mathematician Pythagoras was one of the first to identify important

PYTHAGORAS

mathematical relationships in music. Dividing a string into two parts according to specific ratios, he discovered that particular sonorities would result. Today these consonances are identified as the perfect fourth (4:3), perfect fifth (2:3), and perfect octave (2:1). Beginning in the late Middle Ages, these were the pleasing sonorities that composers sought. But they still don't tell us how such sounds were recorded for posterity in the ancient world.

Our knowledge of the music of ancient Greece is based on only a handful of pieces and fragments; very little has survived after 2,500 years. In addition to the toll that time takes on historical artifacts, the records of music that do exist are meager because there was no known system of notation. Music was performed and transmitted according to the conventions of the time. What we do know about ancient Greek music comes from two important artifacts: the Seikolos Epitaph (music and text inscribed on a tombstone) and a choral ode from a play called *Orestes* by Euripedes. (It is a *choral* ode because it was performed by the chorus, a defining element of ancient Greek drama). One of the great Greek tragedies, *Orestes* tells the story of Orestes, who murdered his father Agamemnon for having committed adultery against his mother.

If the ancient Greeks left only a few scraps of music history, the ancient Romans left us empty-handed. We know virtually nothing of the music performed in ancient Rome during the same period. We

IT'S ALL GREEK TO ME.

NERO

do know that music was an important part of Roman culture, which they largely adopted from the Greeks. Images of instruments and written documents demonstrate that music played an important role in public ceremonies and that emperors were often patrons of the arts. Aside from this, the Romans had little lasting effect on the development of Western musical notation, with the exception of one man after the fall of the Roman Empire: Boethius. In the sixth century C.E., Boethius devised a phonetic system of 15 letters assigned to different pitches. His system eventually became part of modern musical notation.

The Middle Ages not only produced a large body of liturgical (sacred) music, but more importantly, created a system of music dictation that, after several hundred years, evolved into musical notation as we know it today. There was no single, codified means of recording music. Eighth-century Romans recorded on paper the texts used in liturgies, but the accompanying melodies were not written anywhere; they were passed down orally from generation to generation. There were hundreds of chants, and it is unlikely that all of them were transmitted accurately through the centuries. It is a matter of great debate among scholars as to how these melodies were preserved. The consensus is that the most frequently sung melodies were passed on accurately, while variations developed for the less frequently sung chants.

IT'S HARD ENOUGH CREATING A WHOLE NEW LANGUAGE WITHOUT PEOPLE READING OVER YOUR SHOULDER!

Oral transmission was certainly a fallible and unreliable system for the preservation of music, which different people remembered differently. Necessity being the mother of invention, notation, a means for writing down music, was developed over time to accurately record medieval chants. Although there had been earlier and more imprecise attempts at music notation, leading the development of musical notation in the eleventh century was Guido of Arezzo, an Italian Benedictine monk who devised a system based on four lines and three spaces. Guido used this new notational system to record the many chants used in church liturgy. It's important to note that chants were single melodies, without instrumental accompaniment. The vertical placement of small signs called "neumes" (derived from the Latin *neuma*, meaning "gesture") indicated pitch graphically. A neume also indicated the number of pitches assigned to each syllable of text, as well as the contour of the melody. Guide of Arezzo's system (known as staff notation) would eventually lead to the five-line, four-space staff used in modern musical notation. His system was nearly flawless, with one very important exception: there was no method for indicating rhythmic duration.

GUIDO OF AREZZO

While a system for notating music, rudimentary as it was, had been created by about 1100 C.E., musical notation was not nearly as ubiquitous as it is today. Transcribing music proved both laborious and expensive, as everything was copied by hand with quills and ink onto paper or vellum, dried calf-skin used as parchment. Because of this, music was not widely disseminated and many people were musically illiterate. Only members of the highest social class or the clergy might have been able to read music.

Between about 1100 and 1300 C.E., music began to develop from a single line of chant to multiple voices singing simultaneously, which we now call polyphony. Originally, polyphony was achieved by the addition of more voices as a means of ornamenting a single line of chant. By the thirteenth century, these "ornaments" had become an expected part of the music and were no longer considered merely decorative. The development of polyphony was further enabled by simultaneous developments in musical notation (including a few ways to notate rhythmic durations). One of the first means of notating duration in music was through a system of rhythmic modes. There were six modes in all, grouped in short and long notes (called breves and longs) in varying combinations. While this was an important step forward in notation, it still limited composers to a set of specific rhythmic durations.

The solution to this was developed around 1280 by Franco of Cologne. He created a system of rhythmic notation based on the shape of the notes, a characteristic Western music has held onto ever since. Franco's system relied on a simple hierarchy of rhythmic durations, each half as long as the preceding on: the double long, the long, the breve, and the semibreve. This can clearly be seen in modern music notation, which employs whole notes, half notes, quarter notes, and eighth notes, each half as long as the preceding one. By freeing composers from restrictive rhythmic modes, Franconian notation allowed for innovation and variety in the composition of music.

France's Philippe de Vitry (1291–1361) was the leading composer of the fourteenth-century movement called the Ars Nova. This "new art" led to innovations in both rhythm and symbols as employed in musical notation. First, rhythmic notation in the Ars Nova allowed for any rhythmic duration to be divided into either groups of two ("imperfect" duple division) or three ("perfect" triple division). Until that time, the standard in music composition had been for the perfect division of three; now the imperfect division of two became possible. Think of imperfect and perfect divisions as simple and compound, as defined in Chapter 2. Additionally, the semibreve was no longer the smallest possible rhythmic duration; composers in the fourteenth century could subdivide the semibreve into *minims*. Furthermore, symbols were placed at the beginning of staves to indicate the metric division of the music. Called "mensuration signs," these symbols were the predecessors to modern time signatures.

While such innovations were certainly important, they would have gone for naught without ways to duplicate and disseminate music to the masses more efficiently. Copying music by hand (or carving it into blocks of wood) was time-consuming and laborious. Fortunately, Johann Gutenberg perfected a method of movable type around 1440, which allowed for the symbols in musical notation to be combined in any order, rearranged, and reused. A Venetian entrepreneur named Ottaviano Petrucci was among the first to take advantage of this technological innovation when, in 1501, he published the first collection of polyphonic music. Petrucci helped get music into the hands of the masses, creating partbooks that allowed for music to be performed at social gatherings in homes and in churches. Partbooks contained a single part for each voice in a piece of polyphonic music, and were sold in sets containing all of the parts. Business boomed for Petrucci and the music publishing industry, prompting several competitors to establish their own publishing businesses in the sixteenth century.

In short, a great number of people, cultures,

and musical movements contributed to what we know today as musical notation. Eventually the four-line staff created by Guido of Arezzo would be replaced with a five-line staff, and the ancient clefs at the beginning of Gregorian chant lines would become our modern treble and bass clefs. With the invention of the computer, composers now rely much less on sketching and notating music by hand, opting to input their music immediately into music notation software.

III.

SCALES
AND KEYS

Chapter 5:
MAJOR SCALES AND KEYS

NEARLY ALL OF the music in the world is built upon what we call a *scale*, a collection of five to eight pitches arranged in either ascending or descending order. There are many different types of scales used in world music. Although many date back to antiquity, we know the exact origin of only some. While rhythm and pitch are the most basic, fundamental elements of music, the scale is what is what really lets us create music. In modern Western music, scales consist of eight pitches arranged in patterns of whole steps and half steps. There are two main types of scale in Western music: major and minor. Together, they represent what is known as tonal music.

It wasn't until the early Baroque period (1600 – 1750, C.E.) that the concept of "major and minor" (that is, tonality) was truly established. Until then, composers worked primarily with the church modes.

The octave can be divided into twelve equal half steps. This is called the *chromatic scale*, and it essentially represents all pitches. Ascending, the chromatic scale is spelled with sharps; descending, it is spelled with flats. (Remember the enharmonic equivalents we learned about in Chapter 3.) Figure 5.1 shows both the ascending and descending chromatic scale. The scale starts on C in this example, but it can start on any pitch. If you compare the chromatic scale to the piano keyboard, you'll notice that it contains all of the black and white keys within an octave. The chromatic scale is seldom used in the composition of Western music, but it serves as an important starting point for the development of the major and minor scales that *are* prominent in Western music.

Figure 5.1. *Ascending and descending chromatic scales*

Johann Sebastian Bach (1685–1750) is widely considered the greatest composer ever to have lived. He was such a master of composition that he wrote two pieces—a prelude and a fugue—in both the minor and major keys of each pitch of the chromatic scale, for a total of 24 pieces in a collection called *The Well-Tempered Clavier*. Of course, this wasn't enough for Bach; he actually did the same compositional exercise twice and divided the total 48 pieces into *Book I* and *Book II*.

Although most scales are some combination of whole and half steps, occasionally a scale will use an interval larger than a whole step. Scales give music its particular color or flavor, because the unique combination of intervals is then transferred to the melody and harmony. The major and minor scales are both seven-pitch scales containing five whole steps and two half steps, yet they sound strikingly different! In order to understand tonal music, you must remember that the melodic and harmonic patterns of music are the reflection of a pattern of intervals, the scales.

The *major scale* is a seven-pitch scale that consists of five whole steps and two half steps, with the half steps occurring between the third and fourth tones and between the seventh and first tones. When a major scale begins on the pitch C, the scale is simply all of the white keys played sequentially within the octave. In Figure 5.2 you can see that the half steps in a C major scale fall between E and F and between B and C. Compare the musical notation to the keys of a piano, and you'll notice that E and F and B and C are white keys that are immediately adjacent to each other.

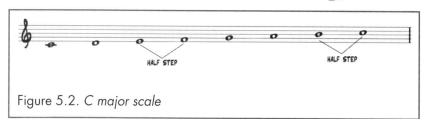

Figure 5.2. *C major scale*

The major scale employs a particular pattern of whole steps and half steps: whole, whole, half, whole, whole, whole, half. This pattern remains true regardless of which pitch you begin on. What gives the major scale such a distinctive, recognizable quality? First, there is the establishment of the **tonic** pitch, which is the foundation of the scale and — by no coincidence — the starting pitch of the scale. You might also think of this as the "home" pitch. The half step between the seventh and first tones of the scale creates a particular pull toward the tonic, and all other pitches want to find their way home to the tonic as well. The seventh tone is called the **leading tone** because it always leads toward the tonic. In many ways, this works like "aural gravity," with the tonic acting as a large object pulling the surrounding objects toward it.

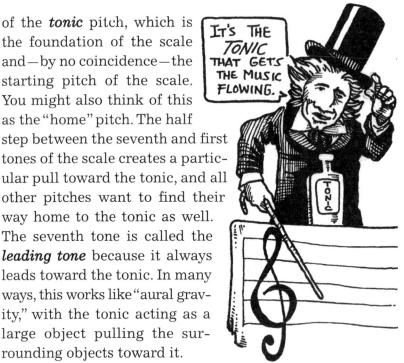

Figure 5.3. *The pattern of whole and half steps that comprise a major scale*

As mentioned above, a major scale can start on any of the pitches of the chromatic scale, and if the pattern of whole steps and half steps remains intact, the result will still be a major scale. For example, if the scale were to begin on the pitch F, it would be necessary to add a flat to the B in order to create the half step between the third and fourth tones and thereby maintain the pattern (Figure 5.4). Similarly, an A-flat major scale requires four flats (one of which is simply to lower the A to A-flat). Figure 5.5 shows the pattern of whole steps and half steps required to make an A-flat major scale, as well as the necessary accidentals.

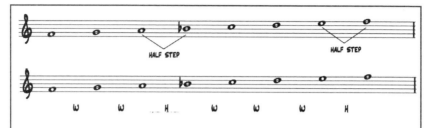

Figure 5.4. *F major scale showing the pattern of whole and half steps*

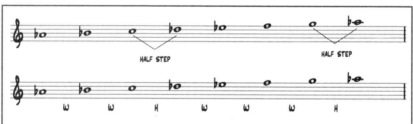

Figure 5.5. A-flat major scale showing the pattern of whole and half steps

Remember that as long as you keep the pattern of whole steps and half steps intact, you can form a major scale beginning on any pitch. The other important piece of information when creating a scale is that the letter names of the pitches must always be sequential. For example, the A-flat major scale in Figure 5.5 uses the pitches A♭, B♭, C, D♭, E♭, F, and G. Even though we can enharmonically

spell B♭ as B# or D♭ as C#, we must use a sequential ordering of the pitches' letter names.

In the case of Figure 5.5, if we were to write an accidental every time we needed one in a piece of music that uses the A-flat major scale, it would clutter the page and be extremely difficult for the performer to read. Because A-flat major always uses a specific set of accidentals (remember, it must contain those accidentals to maintain the pattern of whole steps and half steps), a musical shorthand symbol called a key signature was developed. The **key signature** is placed at the beginning of every staff and is a collection of all the sharps or flats in a given key. It is important to remember that the accidentals of the key signature apply to the entire work and to those pitches *at every octave level*. Figure 5.6 shows the effect of using a key signature for the A–flat major scale. Notice how each of the previous notes that were flatted with an accidental (A, B, D, and E) are now made flat by the key signature.

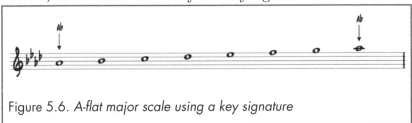

Figure 5.6. A-flat major scale using a key signature

There are a couple of other important points to note regarding accidentals and key signatures. As mentioned in the previous paragraph, the accidentals in the key signature remain in effect throughout a piece of music unless cancelled by a natural (§). The natural, however, along with any other accidental not in the key signature, will apply only until the end of the measure, indicated by a bar line. Additionally, any accidentals not in the key signature placed in front of notes apply to that specific pitch only; unlike key signatures, these accidentals do not affect the same pitch in a higher or lower octave.

The order of the flats or sharps (it can only be one or the other) in a key signature is not haphazard. The flats and sharps must follow a specific sequence that is designed to make the key signature easy to read (and also demonstrates the relationships between keys, which we will learn about later). Figure 5.7 shows the order of sharps for key signatures. Notice that the sharps are always in a specific order. Using A major as an example, the first sharp is F, the second is C, and the third is G. It is not possible to have C-sharp or G-sharp in the key signature without the F-sharp. The order of sharps is always F# – C# – G# – D# – A# – E# – B#.

Additionally, the sharps are always located on specific lines and spaces—this may never be altered. One additional tip for identifying the key associated with the sharp key signatures: the last sharp is always the *leading tone* of the key. In the example of the key signature with four sharps, the last sharp is D-sharp. Because the leading tone is a half step away from the tonic, we know that E, a half step up from D-sharp, is the tonic. With time, practice, and a bit of memorization, you will soon be able to identify these key signatures with ease.

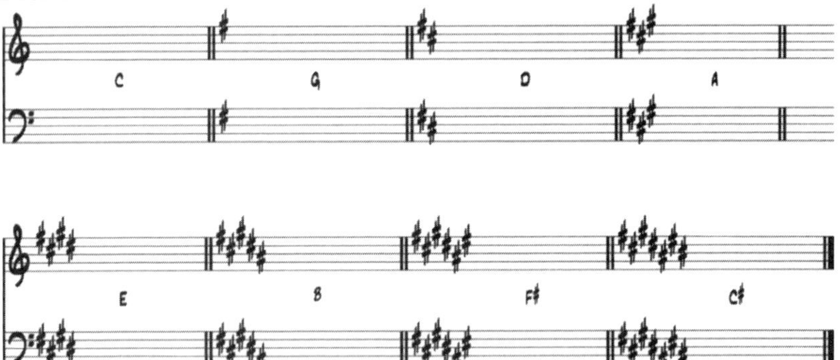

Figure 5.7. *The order of sharps for major key signatures*

Like key signatures with sharps, key signatures with flat also follow a specific order: B♭ – E♭ – A♭ – D♭ – G♭ – C♭ – F♭. You may notice that it is simply the reverse of the order of sharps. Again, the flats are placed on specific lines and spaces, and this too must be memorized. A little trick for identifying the names of major keys that have key signatures with flats is to look at the second-to-last flat of the key signature: this is always the tonic of the key. Of course, the trick works only for key signatures that have at least two flats (you're on your own for F major!). Figure 5.8 shows the order of sharps for major scales with flats in the key signature. Notice that the last three key signatures of both Figure 5.7 and Figure 5.8 are related; they are enharmonic respellings of the same key. C-flat major is the same as B major; G-flat major is the same as F-sharp major; and C-sharp major is the same D-flat major.

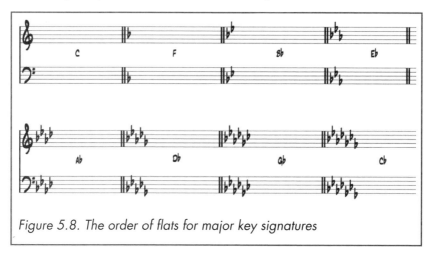

Figure 5.8. The order of flats for major key signatures

One final concept will help tie all of this information together, and that is the *circle of fifths*. The circle of fifths is a diagram that demonstrates that keys are related by the interval of a fifth. Remember that an interval is the distance between two pitches. For example, if we want to know the interval from G down to C, we simply count "G, F, E, D, C" and learn that G down to C is an interval of a fifth. Figure 5.9 demonstrates the circle of fifths for the major keys. Notice that the key signature adds one sharp at a time going clockwise and adds one flat at a time going counterclockwise. Also notice the three keys that share the same keys on the piano, but are enharmonically spelled differently. The circle of fifths is a useful tool because it helps navigate the relationships between keys. Additionally, you will see in Chapter 9 just how important the interval of the fifth is for establishing modern tonal music as we know it!

Figure 5.9. *The circle of fifths for major keys*

Chapter 6:

MINOR SCALES AND KEYS

YOU MAY BE a little worried at this point about the prospect of learning a whole new set of key signatures for the minor keys. Well, there's good news—you've already learned all of the key signatures you need to know. In this chapter, we'll see first how the minor keys are related to the major keys (yes, they *are* related and they share key signatures); then we'll learn how to construct the three different types of minor scales. Although there are three different types, it's important to keep in mind that there is only one key signature for all of them.

There are two different types of relationships between the major keys and the minor keys. The first is the relative relationship; we refer to these keys as the relative major or relative minor. Relative keys share the same key signature and the same set of pitches—the only difference is the starting pitch! When looking at a major scale, we can determine its relative minor by identifying the sixth tone (also known as a scale degree) of the scale. A **scale degree** is a number from one to seven assigned to each of the seven different pitches of a scale. The first pitch is the first scale degree, the third pitch is the third scale degree, and so on. In the instance of F major, we can identify the sixth scale degree as D; therefore, the relative minor of F major is D minor (see Figure 6.1). Again, notice that both scales share the same pitches and the same key signature. The only difference is the starting pitch. This is the simple, yet important, relationship between relative keys. You can think of these keys as existing in pairs, one major and one minor. Another way to identify the relative minor of a major key is to start on the first scale degree (the tonic) and count backwards three half steps. Either method will lead you to the same pitch, which is the tonic of the relative minor.

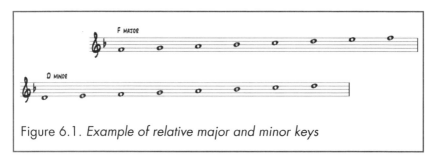

Figure 6.1. *Example of relative major and minor keys*

In addition to the relative relationship between major and minor keys that share the same key signature but different tonic pitches, there is also a parallel major – parallel minor relationship. These keys are also paired, but they are connected in a different way: they share the same tonic pitch but have different key signatures. The difference in key signatures is that the parallel minor has three more flats (or fewer sharps in the case of sharp keys) than its parallel major. In the example of F major, the addition of three flats creates a key signature with a total of four flats (see Figure 6.2).

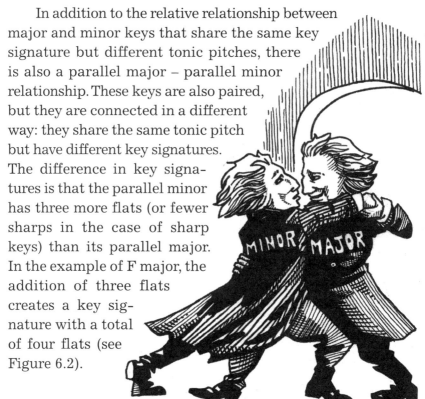

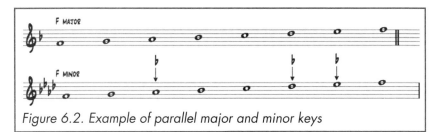

Figure 6.2. Example of parallel major and minor keys

You will notice two important characteristics of the relationship between a major key and its parallel minor. The first is that they share the same tonic but that their key signatures are different. The second is that the third, sixth, and seventh scale degrees are each lowered by a half step. In case you were wondering, this is why the parallel minor of a major key has three additional flats in the key signature. In another example, A major's parallel minor is A minor; A major has three sharps and A minor has no sharps or flats in the key signature. Remember that subtracting sharps is the same as adding flats.

It should be easy enough to find the parallel major from the minor key because they share the same tonic and, therefore, the same letter name. For example, the parallel major of G minor is G major, and the parallel major of D minor is D major. But how does one find the *relative* major of a minor key? There are two ways of doing this, and they are simply the inverse of what you learned for finding the relative minor of a major key: 1) count three half steps *up* from the tonic to arrive at the tonic of the relative major, or 2) simply find the third scale degree of the minor scale, which is the tonic of its relative major. In the instance of F minor, the third scale degree is A♭, which makes A♭ major the relative major of F minor. A♭ major's key signature has four flats, the same as F minor.

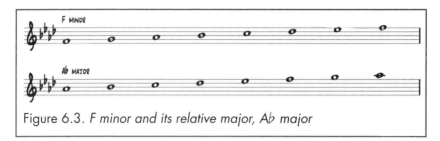

Figure 6.3. *F minor and its relative major, A♭ major*

Figures 6.4 and 6.5 will be helpful to you in associating minor keys with their respective key signatures. Again, remember that these are the same key signatures with the same order of sharps and flats as the major keys!

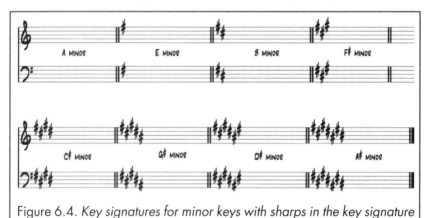

Figure 6.4. *Key signatures for minor keys with sharps in the key signature*

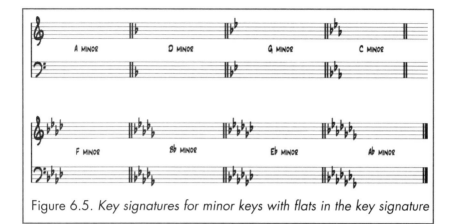

Figure 6.5. *Key signatures for minor keys with flats in the key signature*

Before moving on to learn about constructing the three different types of minor scale, it's worth reviewing the circle of fifths, especially in light of our new knowledge about the relationship between major and minor keys. Get to know Figure 6.6 like your best friend!

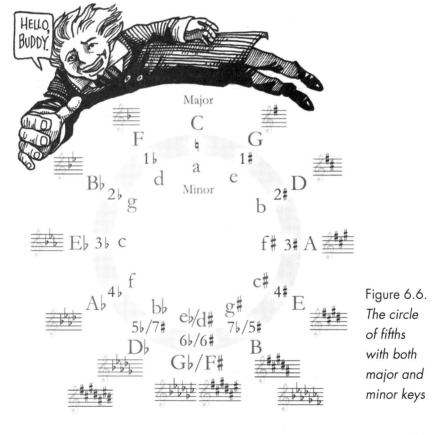

Figure 6.6. *The circle of fifths with both major and minor keys*

It was noted at the beginning of this chapter that there are three types of minor scales. In reality, it is better to think of these as three variants of a single minor scale. The half step between the second and third scale degrees is what gives all variants their minor "flavor." The sixth and seventh scale degrees, however, are fairly unstable, and that is what allows for the variation in minor keys. This instability reflects the fact that, in two of the variants, the sixth and/or seventh scale degrees are borrowed from the parallel major. Composers don't sit down and declare that they will compose a piece in a specific variant of minor; rather, they tend to use elements of all three.

The first type of minor scale, seen in the earlier figures, is called **natural minor**. It is referred to this way simply because it derives naturally from its relative major. It exists without any alterations (and therefore without any added accidentals). In comparison to the major scale, it features flatted third, sixth, and seventh scale degrees. The F minor scale in Figure 6.7 is an example of a natural minor scale.

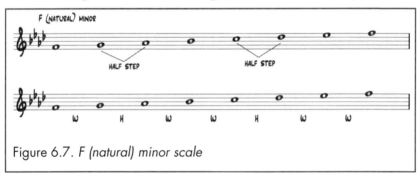

Figure 6.7. F (natural) minor scale

Like the major scale, the natural minor scale is a fixed pattern of whole steps and half steps. Notice, however, that the half steps occur in different places than they do in the major scale. The pattern of whole steps and half steps has also changed: whole – half – whole – whole – half – whole – whole. With the exception of A minor (the relative minor of C major), accidentals are necessary to keep the pattern intact. F minor requires the use of four flats to maintain the pattern necessary for natural minor. Just as in major scales,

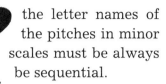

the letter names of the pitches in minor scales must be always be sequential.

If you can play or sing through the F minor scale above, you might notice that it sounds a bit odd at the end, particularly compared with what you are accustomed to hearing at the end of a major scale. The difference is in the interval between the seventh scale degree and the first scale degree at the end of the scale. Instead of being a half step apart, as in a major scale, they are a whole step apart in a natural minor scale. Because the seventh scale degree is a whole step away from the tonic, it is called the *subtonic*, not the leading tone. The lack of a half step between the seventh and first scale degrees results in less of a pull toward the tonic, and the tonic seems to have less gravity than in the major scale.

Composers found a remedy for this: they borrowed the seventh scale degree from the parallel major, thus creating *harmonic minor*. The term will make a bit more sense when we move on to the next unit. For now, you should know that all of the scale degrees of harmonic minor are the same as natural minor except for the seventh scale degree, which is raised a half step to create a leading tone. Composers do this to create stronger harmonies and to cause a greater pull toward the tonic.

Figure 6.8 uses F minor again to demonstrate the alteration needed to create a harmonic minor (and resulting intervals). Notice that there are now three half steps in the scale: between the second and third, fifth and sixth, and seventh and first scale degrees. The seventh scale degree has been raised from E-flat to E-natural; you would not use a sharp to raise the seventh scale degree, because it only needs to be raised a half step. The other result of raising the seventh scale degree to make it the leading tone is a now larger interval between the sixth and seventh scale degrees: an augmented second. While it may look like a regular whole step, the D-flat and E-natural are actually *three* half steps apart, which is why it is called an augmented second. It is often difficult to sing or play because it *sounds* wider than it looks on the staff. This interval also gives the scale a somewhat exotic quality; the augmented second interval is frequently found in Middle Eastern music. We will learn more about intervals in the next chapter.

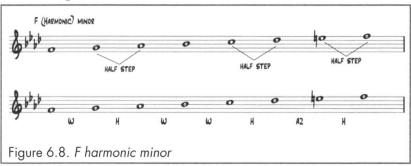

Figure 6.8. *F harmonic minor*

Composers generally try to avoid awkward and difficult intervals in their music. The somewhat awkward and difficult augmented second interval led composers to raise not only the seventh scale degree, but also the sixth scale degree, thereby eliminating the augmented interval. The result of this is known as **melodic minor**. Unlike natural minor and harmonic minor, melodic minor has a scale used for ascending melodies and a different scale for descending melodies. The ascending scale for melodic minor raises both the sixth and seventh scale degrees by a half step, while the descending scale returns them to their "natural" state—the same as in natural minor.

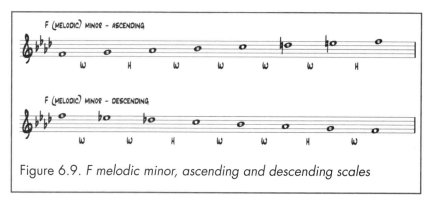

Figure 6.9. *F melodic minor, ascending and descending scales*

Logically, the melodic minor scale is used to make a line sound more fluid, and thus more easily played or sung. You may have noticed already that the only difference between the ascending version of the melodic minor scale and a major scale is the third scale degree! This reinforces the relationship between parallel keys, as well as the borrowing of the sixth and seventh scale degrees from the parallel major. Because the leading tone is generally needed only in melodic passages that move upward, the use of natural minor for the descending scale is suitable for fluidity and playability.

When considering minor scales, remember that you need to look *inside* the music to see which variant of minor is being used and that they are just that—variants of a single minor scale.

ASCEND...
DESCEND...

Chapter 7:
MORE SCALES!

SO FAR WE have covered five scales: the chromatic scale, the major scale, and the three variants of the minor scale. You are likely to encounter a few others, some of which are particularly important in popular music (rock and jazz) as well as folk music. In reality, hundreds of different scales are used throughout the world. However, the five scales that we have already covered—plus four others—are the ones used most often in modern Western music (both popular and classical). This chapter is difficult to place in logical sequence because two of the four other scales deal with intervals we haven't learned about yet. At the same time, it seems appropriate to cover these scales here, after learning about the major and minor scales. It will probably be useful to review the scales in this chapter again after reading the next chapter about intervals.

IF I HAD A SCALE I'D MAKE MUSIC IN THE MORNIN' ... BUT IF I HAD A HAMMER —

The pentatonic scale and the blues scale are important because they form the basis for a large amount of the world's music. A large portion of folk music everywhere is written in the pentatonic scale, while the blues scale is used not only in blues itself, but also in certain styles of jazz and rock. While the ability to read and write both the major and minor scales is the first priority for anyone studying music theory, understanding these additional scales is important to your overall knowledge and musicianship.

The pentatonic scale is one of the oldest in the world, which is likely why so many folk songs use it as their basis. The **pentatonic scale** consists of five tones in an octave. (*Pentatonic* comes from the Greek *penta*, meaning "five"). There are many variations of the pentatonic scale, but the most well-known and widely used is the major pentatonic scale, as in Figure 7.1. Unlike the major and minor scales, the major pentatonic scale has no whole steps and has two intervals greater than a whole step.

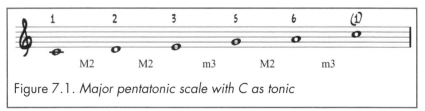

Figure 7.1. *Major pentatonic scale with C as tonic*

The lack of half steps creates a sense of ambiguity with regard to the tonal center. Remember how strongly the leading tone pulls toward the tonic—we don't have this here. Notice also that the half step between scale degrees four and three is also omitted, further weakening the first scale degree's tonal center. The tonal center in pentatonic scales is so obscured that really any of the pitches could serve as the tonic! Fortunately, the starting and ending pitch of a piece of music will usually clue you in to which pitch is the tonic. A number of familiar songs are built on a five-note scale. One notable example is the tune that people sing at midnight on New Year's Eve: "Auld Lang Syne." Look at Figure 7.2 and count the pitches. (Remember to count only letter names, not the total number of pitches used.) Notice that only five

pitches are used: C, D, E, G, and A. Now you can impress your friends and family at the next New Year's Eve party with a quip about "Auld Lang Syne" being based on the pentatonic scale and only using five pitches!

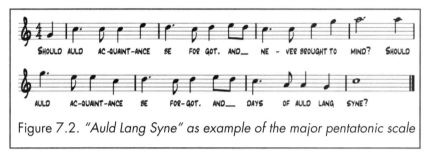

Figure 7.2. *"Auld Lang Syne" as example of the major pentatonic scale*

While the pentatonic scale is pervasive in folk music, it also became popular in classical compositions during the late nineteenth and early twentieth centuries, with composers aiming to emulate the feel of folk or distant historic music. The Russian composer Pyotr Ilyich Tchaikovsky (1840–1893) used pentatonic scales in the first 16 measures of his piece *The Magic Castle*. French composers around the turn of the twentieth century were particularly inspired by the pentatonic scale. Among them were Maurice Ravel (1875–1937) and Claude Debussy (1862–1918). Two of Debussy's more well-known piano compositions use the pentatonic scale almost exclusively: *The Girl with the Flaxen Hair* and *Arabesque No. 1*. The pentatonic scale is also one of the first methods used to teach music notation to children in elementary school, as it is relatively easy to sing and learn.

In addition to the example shown in Figure 7.1, with C as the tonic, the major pentatonic has variants. Another common example uses scale degrees 1, 2, 4, 5, and 6, which would translate to C, D, F, G, and A. Likewise, as demonstrated in Figure 7.3, there is also a minor pentatonic scale with variants. Notice that the minor pentatonic scale uses the *exact same pitches* as the major pentatonic scale! It sounds more "minorish" because pitch A is the first scale degree and because of the leap of a minor third between the first two pitches. While most major pentatonic scales lack half steps, the same is not necessarily true for minor pentatonic scales. Notice in Figure 7.4 that there are two sets of half steps: one between the second and third pitches, and one between the fourth and fifth pitches.

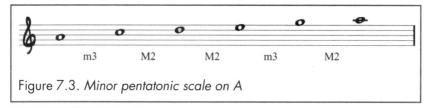

Figure 7.3. *Minor pentatonic scale on A*

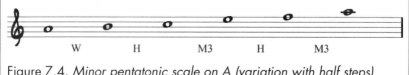

Figure 7.4. *Minor pentatonic scale on A (variation with half steps)*

The other pervasive scale that lies beyond the Western major and minor scales is the blues scales. The **blues scale** is a six-tone scale that combines African pentatonic scales with European major and minor scales. The blues originated as a form of black folk music, created by African slaves and their descendants in the United States. Two of the greatest styles of music to arise from the merging of the two cultures were ragtime and New Orleans jazz.

The blues scale was an attempt to reconcile Western scales with African music, which often featured microtones not found in the 12 pitches of the keyboard. Jazz pianists, in an effort to "find the notes in between the cracks," often will play two adjacent keys that are a minor second apart. The note they are looking for lies somewhere within that minor second interval, but Western music notation (until the twentieth century) had no way of indicating such a pitch. Today, composers regularly indicate intervals smaller than a half step for instruments capable of producing these pitches. (String instruments can, while keyboard instruments, with fixed pitches, cannot). Indeed, many types of world music use scales that divide an octave into smaller intervals than half steps.

The result of the merging of major scales, minor scales, and African scales was the six-tone scale demonstrated in Figure 7.5. Compared to the major scale, you will notice that the blues scale omits scale degrees two and six, flattens scales degrees three and seven, and "splits" scale degree five between a flattened and natural version.

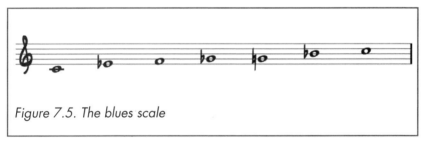

Figure 7.5. The blues scale

The lowered third, fifth, and seventh scale degrees are known as blue notes, because they create added tension when played simultaneously with the non-lowered version of their respective pitches. In practical use, the blues scale is often combined with the major scale, so that there are a total of ten pitches. Think of this as a standard major scale that allows for scale degrees three, five, and seven to be flatted in addition to the seven naturally occurring pitches of the major scale.

ROBERT
JOHNSON

The **blues** (and later the 12-bar blues) took root in the early 1900s in an oppressed and largely illiterate black population. The blues were a cathartic way of expressing personal misery. In contrast to spirituals, which were religious in nature and meant to be sung by a group of people, the blues focused on the individual, were intended to be sung by an individual, and generally excluded the mention of religion or God.

Two other scales should be mentioned, although their use in Western classical music really did not take hold until the twentieth century. The first of these is the whole-tone scale. As you may deduce from the name, the *whole-tone scale* divides the octave into six equal whole steps. It is similar to the chromatic scale in that it lacks any center of gravity. The whole-tone scale also lacks any interval of a perfect fourth of fifth (in relation to the tonic), one of the key components of creating a sense of tonality. If you thought the pentatonic scale was tonally ambiguous, then you should play or sing the whole-tone scale! Although there is no leading tone and the scale lacks the perfect fourth and fifth intervals, it is theoretically possible to establish a tonal center (or tonic) through repetition of a particular pitch. Figure 7.6 shows the only two forms of whole-tone scale that exist. Notice that in order to start and end on the same pitch (in terms of enharmonic spelling), there must be an interval of a diminished third, which sounds identical to a whole step.

Figure 7.6. The whole-tone scale demonstrated in its two forms

Igor Stravinsky (1882–1971) is one of the more famous composers to have used the octatonic scale in his compositions. Among these works was his groundbreaking ballet of 1913, *The Rite of Spring*, which features prominent, striking dissonances (by means of the octatonic scale), along with pounding rhythms and extreme percussiveness. Together, these elements would become known as primitivism. The term is particularly well suited to Stravinsky's ballet, as *The Rite of Spring* dealt with pagan fertility rites in prehistoric Russia. This new musical style was so shocking to the ballet's first audience that they actually booed, hissed, and rioted. During his "Russian Period," Stravinsky also composed *The Firebird* and *Petrushka*, all at the request of ballet impresario Sergei Diaghilev, who founded the Ballet Russes in Paris.

The other scale you should be aware of is the octatonic scale. Like the whole-tone scale, the octatonic scale is a "synthetic" scale in that it was intentionally created in the twentieth century. The **octatonic scale** is a scale of eight pitches that alternate by whole step and half step. There are two versions: the first begins with a whole step, followed by a half step, and so on; the second version begins with a half step, followed by a whole step, and so on. Because of the even distribution of whole steps and half steps, the octatonic scale also lacks a clear tonal center, much like the whole-tone scale. The two versions of the octatonic scale are shown in Figure 7.7.

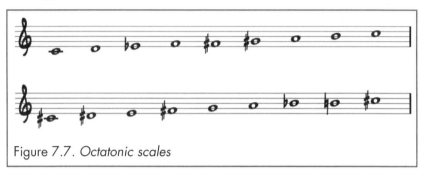

Figure 7.7. *Octatonic scales*

IV.

INTERVALS
AND HARMONY

Chapter 8:

INTERVALS

INTERVALS, AS WE have seen, are the way to measure the distance between pitches. They are extremely important in music theory, providing one of the most fundamental building blocks of notation. At their most fundamental level, the major and minor scales we have been looking at can be understood as patterns of intervals. There are two different kinds of musical intervals, with two different sound qualities: harmonic intervals and melodic intervals. Harmonic intervals occur when two pitches are sounded simultaneously. Melodic intervals occur when two pitches are sounded in succession. Figure 8.1 shows examples of both harmonic and melodic intervals using the same pitches.

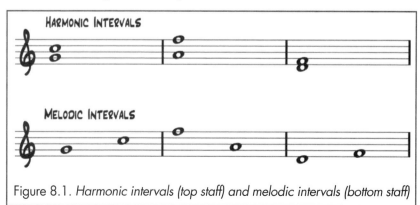

Figure 8.1. *Harmonic intervals (top staff) and melodic intervals (bottom staff)*

Identifying musical intervals is best done in two steps: determining the size of the interval and determining the quality of the interval. The staff makes determining the size relatively easy. All you have to do is count the number of lines and spaces, including the pitches themselves. In the first example, shown in Figure 8.1 (either the melodic or the harmonic intervals), start by counting the first pitch (G) as "1" and continue counting lines and spaces until you reach the second pitch, including the final pitch (C). This will give you the number 4, which tells you that the interval is some quality of a fourth.

The staff also makes it easy to identify the size of intervals, because of their graphic representation on the staff. As shown in Figure 8.2, intervals of a second are always adjacent on the staff, with one pitch on a space (or line) and the other on the adjacent line (or space). Intervals of a third always appear on consecutive lines or spaces. Intervals of a fourth always appear with one pitch on a line and the other on a space, with a line and a space in between them. Intervals of a fifth always appear on spaces with a space in between, or on lines with a line in between.

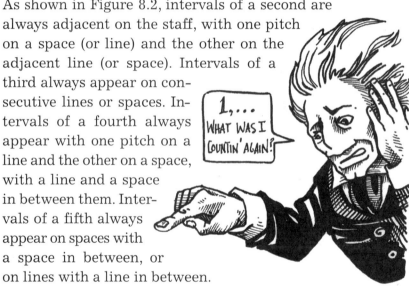

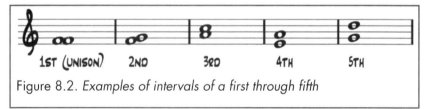

1ST (UNISON)   2ND   3RD   4TH   5TH

Figure 8.2. *Examples of intervals of a first through fifth*

The pattern continues for intervals of a sixth, seventh, and octave (the term for pitches that are eight pitches apart); indeed the intervals continue beyond that (more about those in a moment). Until you can easily and accurately identify the size of intervals at sight, continue counting the lines and spaces, especially for intervals that are larger than a fifth.

The second step in identifying intervals is to determine their quality. This is an important feature, as not all intervals of the same numerical size sound the same. Think back for a moment to the augmented second interval in the harmonic minor scale. A whole step (also known as a major second) is comprised of two half steps, while the augmented second is comprised of three half steps. The number of half steps between pitches is the key to determining the quality of a given interval.

Intervals are described by five different qualities, each with its own letter or symbol: minor intervals (abbreviated with a lowercase *m*, as in m3 for a minor third); major intervals (M); perfect intervals (P); augmented intervals (A or +); and diminished intervals (d or °). The most common intervals occur naturally in scales and harmony; these are the major, minor, and perfect intervals. The quality of perfect can be used to describe only four interval sizes: unison, fourth, fifth, and octave. This is not to say that all of these sizes are *always* perfect. Rather, the quality of perfect can be applied only to them and *not* to intervals of a second, third, sixth, or seventh. Intervals of unison, fourth, fifth, and octave can never be described as being of major or minor quality, but they can be described as augmented or diminished in certain circumstances.

WITH GUYS LIKE US ON THE JOB WHO NEEDS "PERFECT."

Intervals of a second, third, sixth, or seventh are primarily described as major and minor, although they can be augmented or diminished in certain circumstances. They cannot be and are never identified as perfect. Figure 8.3 will help you remember the abbreviations for interval qualities.

Remember how Pythagoras used simple mathematical ratios to define consonances in music of the perfect fourth (4:3), perfect fifth (3:2), and perfect octave (2:1)? These intervals were labeled perfect in the Medieval and Renaissance eras because they were considered the only intervals acceptable for the music to come to temporary or permanent stopping points.

Interval Quality	Abbreviation
Perfect	P
Major	M
Minor	m
Augmented	A or +
Diminished	d or °

Figure 8.3. *Interval qualities and abbreviations*

STOP WHEN I SAY STOP.

There are two ways to determine the quality of an interval. The first is simply to count the number of half steps between pitches. For example, it's easy enough to count two half steps in a major second. But counting the number of half steps in a minor sixth, for example, proves a little more tedious. This method is not preferred, as it involves a lot of memorization and is subject to error. For learners who might prefer it, however, the following table may prove useful in remembering interval qualities.

Interval	# of half steps
P1	0
m2	1
M2	2
m3	3
M3	4
P4	5
A4/d5	6
P5	7
m6	8
M6	9
m7	10
M7	11
P8	12

Table 8.4. *Interval qualities and their respective sizes, in half steps*

The other method is to learn the interval qualities within the context of the major scale by relating them to the tonic pitch. Not only does this method provide a musical context in which to apply the concept, but it also tends to be more accurate (at least if you're very familiar with your scales). Figure 8.5 shows the intervals as they are related to the tonic. Understanding intervals in this fashion will prove extremely helpful once we start examining triads and harmony.

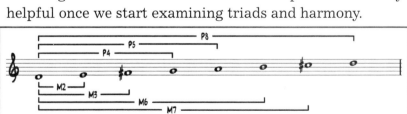

Figure 8.5. *Interval sizes and qualities within the major scale, as related to the tonic*

A short set of rules can help you keep track of the quality of intervals, regardless of whether they are ascending melodic, descending melodic, or harmonic intervals. By knowing them, it becomes easy to make a perfect interval augmented or diminished, major intervals augmented or minor, and minor intervals diminished or major.

- Increasing the size of a perfect interval by a half step results in an augmented interval.

- Increasing the size of a major interval by a half step results in an augmented interval.

- Increasing the size of a minor interval by a half step results in a major interval.

- Decreasing the size of a perfect interval by a half step results in a diminished interval.

- Decreasing the size of a minor interval by a half step results in a diminished interval.

- Decreasing the size of a major interval by a half step results in a minor interval.

Now that you know how to determine the size and quality of an interval, it is important to remember that both must be correct for the interval to be correct; it's not sufficient for one to be correct and the other not. Remember that the size is determined by the total number of letter names in the interval, and the quality is determined by the total number of half steps above or below the first pitch. For example, a perfect fourth requires four letter names between the pitches, as well as five half steps.

You will likely encounter instances where an interval spans a distance larger than an octave. These types are called *compound intervals.* Intervals that span an octave or less are called *simple intervals.* Compound intervals are more difficult to identify by sight because of the larger distance. Like simple intervals, compound intervals can be major, minor, augmented, or diminished. Figure 8.6 shows examples of compound intervals.

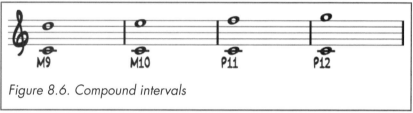

Figure 8.6. Compound intervals

One easy way to identify the size and quality of compound intervals is to reduce them to a simple interval. First, take the higher pitch, then lower it by an octave, and then determine the size and quality of the simple interval. The compound interval's quality will be exactly the same as that of the simple interval; all you need to do is add seven to the size of the simple interval to determine the size of the compound interval. Thus, for example, a major second plus seven results in a major ninth. If this sounds more confusing than it really is, Figure 8.7 explains the relationship graphically.

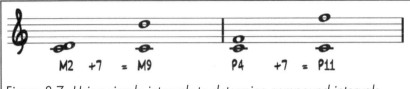
Figure 8.7. *Using simple intervals to determine compound intervals*

Finally, let's consider the relationship between intervals themselves, as they do come in pairs. With the exception of the perfect unison and perfect octave, all simple intervals can be inverted. For example, an augmented fourth (six half steps) pairs with the diminished fifth (six half steps). This might seem a bit confusing at first, but given that they each have six half steps, looking at them on the staff might help make sense of it. The other pairs of related intervals are the following:

Minor second and major seventh
Major second and minor seventh
Minor third and major sixth
Major third and minor sixth
Perfect fourth and perfect fifth

Figure 8.8 shows the relationship of these intervals and their inversions. Notice that with these intervallic relationships, the pitch names are the same!

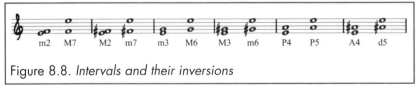

m2 M7 M2 m7 m3 M6 M3 m6 P4 P5 A4 d5

Figure 8.8. *Intervals and their inversions*

Chapter 9

SWEET, SWEET HARMONY

In Western music, the intervallic patterns we now know as scales, both major and minor, form the basis of all intervallic patterns of music. This applies not only to the patterns horizontally (melodically), but also to the patterns that occur vertically (harmonically). **Harmony** is the simultaneous sounding of multiple musical notes, and the basis of harmony is the **chord.** In music theory, we examine harmony not only as the vertical sonorities created in a given moment, but also as progressions of chords through musical time. A chord is formed when three or more pitches are sounded at the same time. (Two pitches are simply an interval). The fundamental chord of harmony is the **triad,** a three-note chord comprised of stacked thirds.

Beyond the triad, there are many possibilities for superimposed thirds; these result in seventh chords, ninth chords, and so on. But for now we will focus on the all-important triad. The triad, like the interval, has four possible qualities: major, minor, augmented, and diminished. The triad consists of a root pitch with two superimposed thirds. The quality of triad is determined by the quality of the thirds that comprise it. The three parts of the chord are identified as the root, the third, and the fifth, and triads are identified according to the letter name of their root combined with their quality. Even when the triad is not in its root position, these names still apply to their respective pitches (see Figure 9.1).

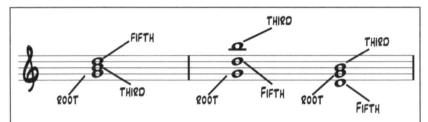

Figure 9.1. *G-major triad in root position (first chord); G-major triad in altered positions (second and third chords)*

By using scales, we can begin to build the foundations of harmony by creating a triad above each of the scale degrees of a major or minor scale. In all major keys, triads built on the first, fourth, and fifth scale degrees are always major; triads built on the second, third, and sixth scale degrees are always minor. We can build a triad based on the seventh scale degree, but because the interval between the root and the fifth is a diminished fifth, the result is a diminished triad. There are no naturally occurring augmented triads within the context of a major key. Figure 9.2 demonstrates the scale degrees and the qualities of the triads built upon them.

Scale degree:	1	2	3	4	5	6	7
Quality:	M	m	m	M	M	m	d

Figure 9.2. *Triads and qualities created within the context of the major scale*

There are several ways of labeling chords. Triads within a key can be identified by the scaled degree upon which they are built (for example, "a triad on scale degree three"), although this is not very common and does not provide a great deal of information. Terms like tonic, subdominant, and dominant are more useful to learn, as they refer both to the scale degree and to the triad that is built upon them. The final way in which musicians refer to triads in the context of a major or minor key is through the use of Roman numerals. Roman numerals are an easy way to indicate a chord's scale-degree position (from I to vii°) and also the chord's quality. An uppercase numeral indicates that the triad is major in quality, while a lowercase numeral indicates that the triad is minor in quality. It is important that you always indicate the key when using Roman numerals; otherwise, the Roman numeral has no musical context! Finally, you can also use letter names to identify chords, using uppercase for major triads and lowercase for minor triads.

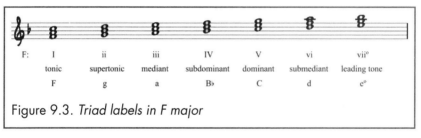

Figure 9.3. *Triad labels in F major*

Building triads in minor keys, unfortunately, is not quite as simple as building them in major keys. The reason for this is the variants of natural minor, harmonic minor, and melodic minor: when you alter a scale degree, you will inevitably alter the quality of the triad built upon it. In natural minor, triads built on the first, fourth, and fifth scale degrees are minor; triads built on the third, sixth and seventh scale degrees are major; and the triad built on the supertonic is always diminished.

Remember the discussion of the subtonic versus the leading tone in minor scales, and how the subtonic doesn't have the same force or pull toward the tonic? This is where harmonic minor gets its name: by raising the seventh scale

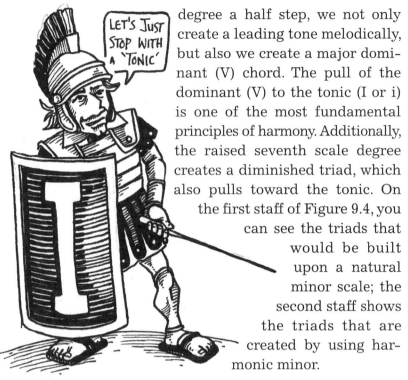

degree a half step, we not only create a leading tone melodically, but also we create a major dominant (V) chord. The pull of the dominant (V) to the tonic (I or i) is one of the most fundamental principles of harmony. Additionally, the raised seventh scale degree creates a diminished triad, which also pulls toward the tonic. On the first staff of Figure 9.4, you can see the triads that would be built upon a natural minor scale; the second staff shows the triads that are created by using harmonic minor.

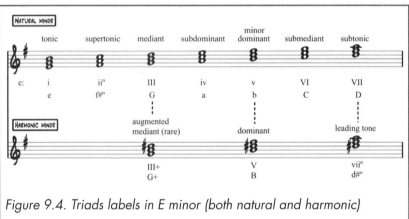

Figure 9.4. Triads labels in E minor (both natural and harmonic)

As previously mentioned, triad qualities are determined by the qualities of the thirds that comprise them. In major triads, the bottom third is major in quality and the upper third is minor in quality. In minor thirds it is the inverse: the bottom third is minor in quality and the upper third is major in quality. Augmented triads are comprised of two major thirds, while diminished triads are created with two minor thirds. This is an easy and quick way to double-check that your triad is the quality you think it is.

For example, if you want to build a major triad on the pitch A (the root), add a C# above it to create a major third (four half steps above) and then an E above that (a minor third higher than the C#. The result is a major triad, and the interval between the root and the fifth is a perfect fifth. To create a minor triad using the same root, the third of the triad would be C (three half steps above to create a minor third), and the fifth would be E (the interval between C and E being a major third). You can use this process to create triads of any quality on any pitch, as long as you use the proper quality of thirds.

Sometimes you will encounter a triad in an altered form. The spacing may be wider, or perhaps the lowest-sounding pitch is not the root of the chord. Remember that when the root of the chord is the lowest-sounding pitch, the chord is in root position. If any other member of the chord is the lowest-sounding pitch, it is said to be inverted. With triads there are two—and only two—possibilities of inversion. First inversion is when the third of the triad is the lowest-sounding pitch; second inversion is when the fifth of the triad is the lowest-sounding pitch. When

NOW THAT'S SOME HARMONIC WRANGLIN' FER YA!

a chord is inverted, the remaining two chord members may be in any order—the only thing that matters is which chord member is lowest-sounding.

ROOT POSITION   FIRST INVERSION   SECOND INVERSION

Figure 9.5. F-major triad in root position, first inversion, and second inversion

WHEN I'M INVERTED LIKE THIS I DON'T KNOW WHETHER TO LEAF OUT OR GROW A CARROT.

As previously mentioned, it is possible to extend tertian harmonies beyond the triad by superimposing additional thirds. In most music, this involves adding just one more third, called the seventh of the chord. This is a logical name for the chord member, as it is a seventh above the root (just as the third and fifth are respective intervals above the root). Like chords in

One of the best tools for practicing your analytical skills is a church hymnal. Hymns are wonderful because their harmonies are usually very straightforward and because they rarely use non-diatonic chords (chords outside those formed by the key that is being used). Of course, most hymns are written for four voices—soprano, alto, tenor, and bass—and triads have only three pitches. So how can this be? When there are four voices, there are rules for deciding which member of the triad should be sung in two voices. When a triad is in root position, the root should always be doubled. When a triad is in first inversion, usually the root is doubled, although it is permissible to double the fifth and occasionally the third. When a triad is in second inversion, the fifth is always doubled. Grab a hymnal and see if the composers of the hymns followed these rules!

hymns, there are now four notes in the chord; however, they are four *different* notes. The most frequently encountered seventh chord is known as the **dominant seventh chord.** The dominant seventh chord is a seventh chord built on the major triad of the V chord (in both major and minor), and it is written as V⁷. A dominant seventh chord is also called a major-minor seventh chord, which might help you remember how to spell it. It consists of a *major* triad with a *minor* seventh added above the root. Figure 9.6 shows several examples of dominant seventh chords in root position.

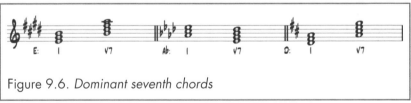

Figure 9.6. *Dominant seventh chords*

The dominant seventh chord is particularly strong because it contains two tendency tones. **Tendency tones** are pitches within a scale that have a strong tendency to move toward a specific adjacent pitch. The leading tone is a tendency tone because of its strong desire to move upward to the tonic. In a dominant seventh chord, the leading tone of the scale is the third of the chord. The seventh of the chord is a tendency tone because it is the fourth scale degree, and the fourth scale degree wants to resolve downward to the third scale degree, particularly in major keys when they are separated by only a half step.

Because seventh chords have four different chord members, there are four possible positions, three of which are inversions. When the root of the chord is the lowest-sounding pitch, it is in root position. When the third of the chord is the lowest-sounding pitch, it is in first inversion. When the fifth of the chord is the lowest-sounding pitch, it is in second inversion. And when the seventh of the chord is the lowest-sounding pitch, it is in third inversion. Figure 9.7 shows examples of each inversion, this time in the four-voice "hymn" style.

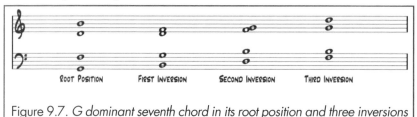

Root Position   First Inversion   Second Inversion   Third Inversion

Figure 9.7. *G dominant seventh chord in its root position and three inversions*

While a bit beyond the scope of a beginning music theory book, it is worth mentioning that seventh chords may have other qualities. You can form a seventh chord with any triad from either the major or the minor scale simply by adding one more third to the chord. Only the seventh chord formed on the fifth scale degree, however, is a dominant seventh chord.

I CAN'T EXPLAIN THIS STRANGE ATTRACTION I FEEL.

V.

PUTTING (MUSIC) THEORY INTO PRACTICE

Chapter 10:
WRITING HARMONIES

THIS CHAPTER DEALS primarily with the concept of *tonal music*, or tonality, a concept that most musicians (and music listeners) take for granted. The idea of tonal music has become so ingrained in Western culture that it's almost difficult to describe, even for trained musicians. Essentially, tonality is what arises from the melodic and harmonic elements drawn from the major and minor scales. But tonality is much, much more than that. It's the way that the members of the scales interact with each other (such as the tendency tones mentioned in the previous chapter). There seems to be a hierarchy of pitches, each rotating around and eventually leading to a central pitch (the tonic) and each having its own level of importance. Indeed the idea of a musical hierarchy extends beyond scale degrees to the harmonies that are built upon them, with the dominant/tonic relationship assuming the most important role in the harmonic hierarchy.

Richard Wagner (1813–1883) was an outstanding composer of German opera who, through his development of harmonies that contradicted traditional harmonic progression, inspired composers such as Gustav Mahler, Arnold Schoenberg, and Alban Berg to abandon tonality completely. One of Wagner's most well-known operas, *Tristan und Isolde*, is notable for his repeated use of dissonant chords that move to other dissonant chords, instead of resolving as expected. He also developed the leitmotiv, a musical thought or motive that represents a character or idea in the opera. If you're a fan of epic trilogies like Tolkien's *The Lord of the Rings*, you might enjoy Wagner's *Der Ring des Nibelungen*. Commonly called the *Ring Cycle*, it is an epic four-opera cycle based loosely on Norse sagas and features approximately 15 hours of music! You're likely already familiar with a bit of the *Ring Cycle*: the famous "Ride of the Valkyries" tune is from the third act of the second opera of the cycle, *Die Walküre*.

In all tonal melodies in the Western modern common practice (at least the ones that are well-written), there is an intrinsic buildup of tension followed by a release; the same can be said for harmonic progressions. Through this pattern of tension and resolution, the harmonic hierarchy creates a sense of forward motion. The strongest combination of tension and release is the dominant-tonic relationship. Without a doubt, the most frequently used harmonic progression in Western music is the movement from the dominant (V) to the tonic (I). The relationship between these two harmonies is such that they alone can establish tonality—and therefore the key of a piece of music.

How can the gravitational pull of the dominant toward the tonic be so strong? Think back to the *circle of fifths*. Notice that all the keys in the circle are a perfect fifth apart. In and of itself, this is like a ball dropping from five feet in the air (the dominant) and hitting the ground (the tonic). The dominant triad includes the supertonic, which wants to resolve to either the first or third scale degree. And then, as we know, the leading tone desperately wants to resolve upward to the tonic. If the dominant is a seventh chord, that fourth tone increases the tension further with a desire to resolve downward to the third scale degree. With the aggregate tension of all the pitches in the dominant harmony, it's no wonder that there is a real sense of forward motion when they finally resolve to the tonic!

German composer **Arnold Schoenberg** (1874–1951) might be the most infamous composer of the twentieth century. Because of the increased use of unresolved dissonance in late nineteenth-century music, Schoenberg felt that the need for a tonal center was arbitrary and abandoned the system of tonality that this book is teaching you! The result was atonality. One of his most famous innovations in atonal composition was the twelve-tone row. Schoenberg took the twelve pitches of the chromatic scale and assigned a number to each of them. He then put the pitches into a matrix that offered a number of possible combinations. The most striking feature of the twelve-tone row was that no pitch could be repeated until all the others had been presented. This compositional methodology eventually became known as serialism, and it led to composers serializing not only pitches, but such other musical elements as rhythms, dynamics, and articulations.

Schoenberg and his students Alban Berg and Anton Webern (collectively known as the "Second Viennese School") are also well known for their use of Sprechstimme in their vocal compositions. German for "spoken voice," Sprechstimme calls upon the performer to merely approximate pitches with the spoken voice; it can be likened to speaking in a singsongy manner. In case you're wondering, the "First Viennese School" was comprised of musical giants Wolfgang Amadeus Mozart, Joseph Haydn, and Ludwig van Beethoven.

RELEASE THE DISSONANCE!

SCHOENBERG

If you're questioning whether a piece of music can truly be written with only two chords, Figure 10.1 offers an example that should prove it to you! "Mary Had a Little Lamb" might seem a bit juvenile for this text, but it's perfect for illustrating this point. It's very common for folk songs and nursery rhymes to employ only a very few chords—in this case just two—as their simplicity makes them perfectly suited to the population at large (in the case of folk songs) and to children (in the case of nursery rhymes). Take a look at the music on your own. Notice how the melody itself uses scale degrees that correspond to the underlying harmonies. Sing through the melody in your head and stop halfway through. It feels incomplete, doesn't it? Now sing through the melody again, this time stopping on the penultimate word ("as"). That strong desire you have to finish the song is the gravitational pull of the dominant to the tonic. (OK, if you can't stand it any longer, go ahead and finish the song!)

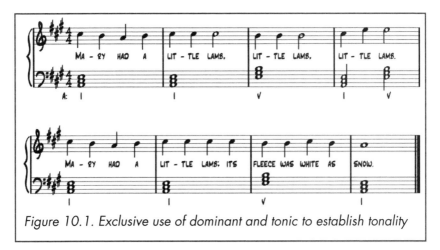

Figure 10.1. Exclusive use of dominant and tonic to establish tonality

This example, which is the most basic, demonstrates a chord progression. A chord progression is the alternation between tension and resolution, between activity and resting. When you stopped halfway through or on the penultimate note of "Mary Had a Little Lamb," you were stopping on the dominant, which has a sense of activity. The music had a strong urge to move forward. The very beginning and the very end of the song, which feature tonic harmonies, are the center of gravity. There is no innate urge to press forward (although if you were to compose a song with only the tonic as harmony, your listeners would probably urge you to move on!). The forward movement and alternation of tension and resolution are supported by three of the characteristics of music described at the beginning of this book: melody, harmony, and rhythm.

The melody in

"Mary Had a Little Lamb" has its own forward motion. It begins with a downward contour and proceeds to an upward contour in the first measure. The melody keeps moving upward and upward, like a balloon, to the fifth scale degree at the end of the fourth measure. Then the balloon pops, and the melody starts again as it did at the beginning. Finally it finds its way home to the tonic in the last measure. The height of the pitch in the fourth measure really has a sense of downward pull—the melody feels as though it must return down; staying that high or continuing higher is not a comfortable option. The harmony, by this point, is pretty straightforward. Notice that those moments of tension in the melody coincide with use of the dominant harmony, which is the most active harmony. The rhythm supports these moments of tension and release through short and long rhythmic passages. Notice how the quarter notes move the melody along, while the longer note values (half note in the fourth measure and whole note in the final measure) serve as resting points. The resting point in the fourth measure says, "Okay, keep on going!" while the resting point in the last measure says, "Okay, we can stop here."

While you may be amazed at how deeply one can

analyze a song as simple as "Mary Had a Little Lamb," you're probably ready to move beyond two-chord progressions. So let's add a third chord to the mix. In the vast majority of three-chord progressions, the third chord is the subdominant. The gravitational pull between IV and I is not nearly as strong as the pull between V and I. The subdominant is a perfect fourth away from the tonic, which does give it some level of activity. Remember that the interval of a perfect fourth is the inversion of a perfect fifth; this is why the IV chord has some degree of gravitational pull toward the tonic. In order of most restful to most active, we have the tonic, the subdominant, and then the dominant, which makes I–IV–V a suitable and common chord progression. The subdominant, in a way, acts as an intermediary that reduces the tension. You can think of the subdominant as the therapist in marriage counseling; the tension will always be there, but it's slightly lessened with the intervention of the therapist.

There are two patterns of three-chord progressions in which the subdominant usually appears: I–IV–V–I and I–IV–I–V–I. In the first pattern, the subdominant raises the tension a notch; the dominant then raises the tension another notch before returning to the tonic, which releases the tension. In the second pattern, the tension is prolonged. The subdominant raises the level of tension but then yields to the tonic; the dominant then raises the tension to an even higher level before eventually yielding to the tonic.

You might be wondering how many songs have been written with just these three simple chords. Twenty? Thirty? Try hundreds, maybe even thousands (if we include ones that never became popular). Perhaps the most recognizable form of chord progression in Western music, the 12-bar blues has served as the harmonic foundation for many, many songs. Examples include Elvis Presley's "Hound Dog," Little Richard's "Tutti Frutti," Louis Prima's "Jump, Jive, and Wail," and "In the Mood," made famous by the Glenn Miller Orchestra.

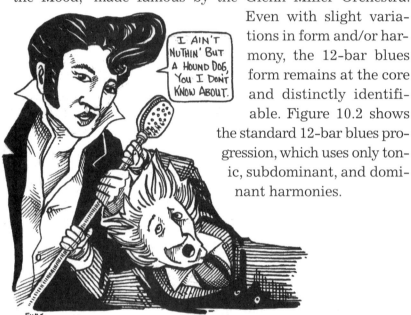

Even with slight variations in form and/or harmony, the 12-bar blues form remains at the core and distinctly identifiable. Figure 10.2 shows the standard 12-bar blues progression, which uses only tonic, subdominant, and dominant harmonies.

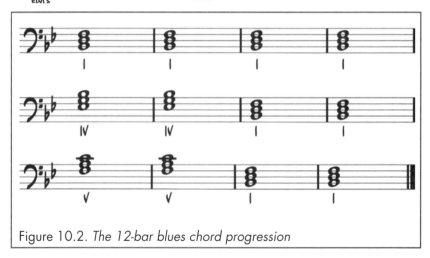

Figure 10.2. *The 12-bar blues chord progression*

You might be wondering what to do with the other four chords that are built upon the scale degrees of the major and minor scales. One of the most important concepts to keep in mind is that chords like to move in intervals of a fifth. In a way, it's like the other chords want to enjoy the strong V–I relationship that the dominant and tonic enjoy (although no other harmonic relationship is as strong as that one). For example, it would be logical for the vi chord to move to the ii chord and then for the ii chord to move to V and then the V to resolve to I.

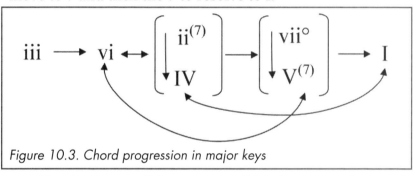

Figure 10.3. Chord progression in major keys

The figures on this page should help you understand the ways in which tonal music usually progresses in both classical and popular music (only *usually* because there are many instances where composers/songwriters don't follow this type of progression). Figure 10.3 shows the possible chord progressions in major keys, while Figure 10.4 shows the possible chord progressions in minor keys.

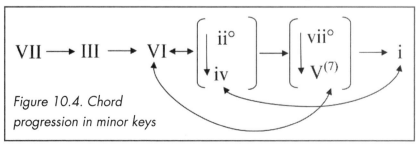

Figure 10.4. Chord progression in minor keys

In minor keys, note that there is an option of using the VII chord (which occurs in natural minor) or the vii° chord (which occurs in harmonic minor). Finally, it's important to understand that I can go to any chord it wants! These figures will prove invaluable as you analyze music or begin composing music of your own.

Chapter 11:
WRITING MELODIES

NOW THAT YOU have a solid understanding of the foundations of music theory, let's take a look at how one goes about writing a piece of music. While some harmonies are memorable in popular music, most of the greatest works are known for their melodies. The best songwriters know how to write a melody that will play over and over again in your head, yet won't sound trite or repetitious. How do they accomplish this? Is it sheer luck or innate talent? Or are there particular techniques that make a melody memorable? In all honesty, it is likely a combination of talent and technique, but it is possible for anyone with an understanding of music theory to write a convincing melody.

There are several aspects to consider when writing a melody.

Composers of popular music who have been known for their great melodies include Henry Mancini, Stevie Wonder, Billy Joel, Elton John, and many others. Of course, there were a few classical composers whose melodies remain familiar today. Beethoven's *Ode to Joy* is frequently sung as a hymn and is the official anthem of the European Union. And, of course, Handel wrote a pretty catchy tune with his "Hallelujah Chorus" from *Messiah*.

CONJUNCT MOTION...

DISJUNCT MOTION !

The first is the contour, or general shape. Most melodies feature stepwise motion (that is, moving whole or half steps along the pitches of the scale), with occasional skips of a third or fourth. This stepwise motion is also known as **conjunct motion**. Occasionally there might be a jump of a larger interval (called a leap). A melodic passage that is "jumpy" and features lots of skips and/or leaps is said to have **disjunct motion**.

Two other aspects that one must consider when writing for an instrument or voice are range and tessitura. *Range* refers to the full span of pitches that a musical work encompasses. Songs with very wide ranges are difficult for all but the best singers to perform, while songs with narrow ranges are more accessible for amateur singers. While instruments tend to have much wider ranges than voices, it is important for a melody to fit the range of the instrument that will be playing it. For example, the lowest playable note for a violin is the G below middle C. Therefore it would be silly to compose a piece for violin in which the pitches go lower than that; even one instance of a pitch outside an instrument's range is unacceptable. *Tessitura* is the general area of pitch (high, middle, low) where the melody tends to lie. Melodies that stay very high or very low for an extended period of time are difficult to sing or play. In composing a melody, try to stay primarily in a middle register, and then selectively move into higher or lower registers based on the song's climax, depiction of the text, or at stopping points.

What makes a song memorable are the motives in its melody. A *motive* (sometimes called a motif, or in popular music a "hook") is the musical germ of your melody. The motive can be tied closely to the rhythm, or it can simply be the intervallic relationships in the tune. A motive might be a single note intrinsically linked to the rhythm (obviously the note must repeated), or it might be two notes, three notes, or four notes. Regardless of the number of pitches in the motive, it's important to develop it and keep it fresh. There are a number of ways that composers take a motive and really turn it into something special.

THE HOOK GETS RIGHT IN YOUR, UH, "HEAD."

Beethoven's Fifth Symphony— "Dum dum dum duuuuuuum."
If you aren't familiar with this music (I would venture to assume that most people have heard it, even unknowingly), then grab a CD or go online and listen to the beginning of Beethoven's Fifth Symphony. This guy really knew how to take an excruciatingly simple motive (four notes, three of which are repeated and the fourth simply a major third lower) and squeeze every drop of musical possibility from it. He repeats it at a lower pitch level; then he repeats it at a higher pitch level.

He shortens it; he lengthens it. He writes it using the minor scale; then he reprises the motive using the major scale. When you're listening to any music—whether classical, jazz, or popular—see if you can latch onto the main musical motive and count how many times it reappears throughout the work.

Chapter 12:
THE SYNTAX OF MUSIC

Now that we've covered pitches, rhythms, scales, harmony, and melody, it's time to see how music is put together with regard to form. In the vast majority of compositions, music does not flow freely from one idea to the next without direction or form. The form of music has structure, much as the design of a building does. Like an architectural plan, a musical structure can be divided into large sections, and then subdivided into smaller and smaller parts. Analogously, an architectural structure might be divided into wings, then wings into floors, floors into rooms, and so on. We can do the same thing with the structural components in music.

The basic unit of musical syntax is the *phrase.* Another useful analogy can be made with language. Consider the following: musical phrases are like sentences, and all sentences eventually come to a stopping point. That stopping point is identified by some form of punctuation, with varying degrees of strength and completeness. For example, a sentence ending with a question mark sounds different from one ending with a period or an exclamation mark. In music, the "punctuation marks" are referred to as *cadences*— temporary or permanent stopping points in a musical phrase. Cadences, like sentences, have different feelings of strength and completeness. Some bring a phrase to a definite close, while others suggest the

WHERE'S THE PHRASE? 'CAUSE I'VE ALREADY GOT MY CADENCE.

need to continue on. Cadences occur both throughout a piece of music and at the very end.

The strongest musical punctuation is known as the authentic cadence. An *authentic cadence* is marked by a move from the dominant to the tonic (V–I in major keys or V–i in minor keys) at a point of rest. However, because all cadences occur at the end of a musical phrase, a move from the dominant to the tonic in the middle of a phrase is *not* a cadence. One good sign that you've reached a cadence is that the stopping point occurs on a longer rhythmic note value. There are two types of authentic cadence: perfect and imperfect. In the *perfect authentic cadence* (abbreviated PAC), both the dominant and tonic chords are in root position, and the uppermost voice (e.g., the soprano in a four-part hymn) moves from scale degree two to one, or from seven to one. Think of the PAC as firm and strong as a period or exclamation point. The *imperfect authentic cadence* (abbreviated IAC) is analogous to a semi-colon; the musical thought is complete, yet it longs for a bit more information. In the imperfect authentic cadence, either or both of the chords are in inversion *and/or* the uppermost voice does not move from scale degree two or seven to one.

Sometimes a musical phrase is left open-ended, like a question begging to be answered. The musical equivalent of a question mark is the *half cadence* (abbreviated HC). The word "half" tells us that the musical idea has not come to an end, but must continue on to another phrase in order to have a sense of completion. We achieve this through a musical phrase that ends on the dominant. Do you remember how "Mary Had a Little Lamb" felt incomplete when you stopped singing halfway through? That's because you reached a half cadence. The penultimate chord and final chord of the song, however, formed a perfect authentic cadence. (Notice how you didn't feel the need to continue singing once you reached the end.) Although there are instances of dominant harmony throughout "Mary Had a Little Lamb," you must remember that cadences occur *only* at the end of musical phrases. In the case of this song, there are two musical phrases: one ending with a half cadence and one ending with a perfect authentic cadence. Here's the music again to refresh your memory.

Two other cadences occur frequently in music. Unfortunately, there are no grammar analogies to help explain them. One is the **deceptive cadence** (abbreviated DC). Some music theorists refer to it as the "one more time!" cadence, because it begs for the previous musical phrase to be repeated until brought to a proper close (with an authentic cadence). How does the deceptive cadence achieve this? Upon reaching a point in the music when the listener expects some sort of authentic cadence (V–I), the cadence begins with the dominant but deceives the listener by moving to a chord other than the tonic. (The substitution of vi for I is the most common deception). By going to the "wrong" chord, the music typically repeats the phrase and ends on the "right" chord (the tonic) at the end of the phrase.

The last cadence we need to learn about is the ***plagal cadence.*** This one is likely to be familiar to churchgoers especially: the IV–I motion that makes the cadence plagal is the same chord combination sung to the syllables of "Amen" at the end of a hymns or other pieces of church music. This cadence, while not open-ended in nature, is not nearly as strong as the authentic cadence. For that reason, it usually follows a final perfect authentic cadence.

At the phrase level (analogous to a sentence or paragraph), one of the most important musical forms is the period. A ***period*** is a musical unit consisting of two phrases. The first phrase, called the ***antecedent***, is musically inconclusive (usually ending with a half cadence). The second phrase, called the ***consequence***, offers a more conclusive end (usually a perfect authentic cadence). The cadential structure is important in periods, but the musical/melodic material is equally important because it distinguishes the two different types of periods. A parallel period features two phrases of the same musical material (a and a'); the first phrase ends inconclusively with a half cadence or imperfect authentic cadence, and the second phrase ends conclusively with a perfect authentic cadence.

A contrasting period features two

AND THERE'S MORE?

phrases of contrasting musical material (a and b), but it, too, features the inconclusive and conclusive cadential structure.

Continuing the grammar analogy, multiple related sentences are combined to form a paragraph. Multiple related paragraphs form a chapter, and the aggregation of chapters form a book. Musical compositions can be divided in a similar way. For example, a symphony typically has four large sections called movements. The movements have a form or structure of their own, and these have been consistent throughout music history.

Binary and ternary forms are common in virtually every genre of music. *Binary form*, as you can guess from its name, is a two-part form that is also known as AB form. It consists of two roughly equal sections of music that are contrasting in musical material. The sections are harmonically closed, meaning that you could play either A or B without the other and the music would sound complete. *Ternary form* is a three-part form (ABA), again with harmonically closed sections and a contrasting B section. The A section is usually repeated verbatim. The middle ground between binary and ternary forms is called the rounded binary form. *Rounded binary form* is a two-part form that brings back a portion of the A section at the end to "round off" the piece. It is abbreviated ABA', with A' representing the portion of A that comes back at the end of the B section. The B section, again contrasting in musical material, is

usually left harmonically open. That is, the B section in rounded binary form usually features a half cadence midway to lead in to the return of A material.

Three-part forms are frequently found in classical music, especially one known as sonata form. **Sonata form** is a three-part form that developed in the Classical period and continued

The term *sonata* has been used broadly since the sixteenth century, and its meaning has changed over time: sonata comes from the Italian *sonare*, which means "to sound." In the Baroque period (roughly 1600 to 1750), the sonata was a piece of music composed for one or two treble instruments, accompanied by bass instruments and keyboard (the latter collectively known as *basso continuo*). There were two different types of sonata: sonata da chiesa (sonata of the church) and sonata da camera (sonata of the chamber). Both the *sonata da chiesa* and *sonata da camera* consisted of four dance-style movements. During this time, the term sonata was also applied to compositions for solo keyboard instrument, usually the harpsichord.

through the Romantic period. It is considered to be one of the most important formal structures in the history of music. Its three parts consist of the exposition, the development,

During the Classical period, sonata would become the designated term for multimovement works for solo piano or solo instrument plus piano accompaniment. The sonata followed a prescribed multimovement form: a fast movement that employed a three-part form (now known as sonata form); a second, slow movement; and a third fast movement, often labeled Finale. Eventually this structure would be extended to symphonies and string quartets, which usually followed a four-movement structure: a fast movement in sonata form; a second, slow movement; a third movement in a lively dance form; and a finale in a faster tempo. Symphonies and string quartets did not always follow this structure, however, because great composers like Franz Joseph Haydn (known as the "father" of both the symphony and the string quartet) were always seeking to innovate in the use of classical structures!

PAPA!

HAYDN

and the recapitulation, and it can be likened to the rounded binary form. The *exposition* presents a primary theme in the key of the composition, and then moves by means of a transition (called a bridge) to a secondary theme in a different key. The *development* does what its name implies: this section takes musical material from the primary and secondary themes and presents it in new ways (fragmented, expanded, etc.). The development also moves through a number of keys (usually both major and minor) before ending on a prolonged half cadence. The half cadence at the end of the development is on the dominant

of the home key, which sets up the recapitulation. The **recapitulation** is the return of the music from the exposition. The primary difference is that the music of the secondary theme is also presented in the home key, so that the piece can come to a close in it.

EPILOGUE

WHILE IT WOULD be nearly impossible to cover every form found in classical music, we have looked at some of the most widely used: binary, ternary, rounded binary, and sonata form. Likewise, it would be impossible to cover every aspect of harmony, melody, timbre, texture, and rhythm in an introductory music theory book. What this book *does* provide is the tools to start understanding the music in front of you and begin studying, reading, and composing music of your own. Hopefully you will be inspired to continue your study of music theory.

One of the essential elements of learning music (like learning a new language) is regular, daily practice. A quick search of the Internet will turn up hundreds of worksheets in which you can review the knowledge and practice the skills you've learned in this book. Another way to reinforce the skills you've acquired so far is to practice them at the piano. If you don't own one, a small electronic keyboard can be purchased at minimal cost. Finally, if you enjoyed the tidbits of music history in this book, consider reading its companion volume, *The History of Classical Music For Beginners*.

If you absolutely love this "music theory stuff" and are eager to learn more, there are many textbooks on the market that will not only lead you to a deeper understanding of the material covered in this book, but also teach you new and more advanced concepts, all the way up to the music of the twentieth century. Such volumes will likely cost a lot more than this one, but they are worth the investment for the serious student of music theory. As with any art, the sky is the limit as to what you can create and learn about music.

GLOSSARY

Accidentals: symbols used to identify pitches as higher or lower than previously indicated

Bar line: a line on the staff that divides the staff into measures according to the meter

Beat: the underlying pulse in music that is steady and ever-present

Binary form: a two-part (AB) form consisting of two contrasting sections

Blues scale: a six-tone scale that combines African pentatonic scales with European major and minor scales

Clef: the symbol placed at the beginning of a staff to identify the pitches of the lines and spaces

Chord: the simultaneous sounding of three or more pitches

Chromatic scale: the division of an octave into its twelve, equal half steps

Compound interval: an interval that spans more than an octave

Compound meter: a meter whose beat subdivides into three parts

Conjunct motion: melodic movement primarily by steps

Development: the second part of the sonata form, in which musical material from the exposition is reworked in new ways and combinations while wandering through a variety of keys

Disjunct motion: melodic movement by skips and/or leaps

Dominant seventh chord: a major-minor seventh chord built on the fifth scale degree

Duration: the length of time a sound exists in musical time

Dynamic level: the degree of softness or loudness of a given sound

Enharmonic equivalency: two pitches that are spelled differently but sound the same pitch

Exposition: the first part of the sonata form, in which two different themes are presented.

Flat: lowers a pitch one half-step

Grand staff: two staves connected by a brace; used primarily for piano music, choral music, or any other music where the range of pitches is too wide for a single staff

Harmonic minor: a seven-pitch minor scale starting on the sixth scale degree of its parallel major. Scale degrees three and six are flatted, but the seventh scale degree is raised to create a leading tone.

ALL GOOD TO KNOW.

Harmony: the simultaneous sounding of multiple musical notes

Key Signature: the collection of all the sharps or flats in a given key placed at the beginning of every staff

Leading tone: the seventh tone of a scale that is a half step below the tonic

Ledger lines: the small lines added below or above a staff to extend its range in either direction

Interval: the distance between two pitches

Major scale: a seven-pitch scale that consists of five whole steps and two half steps, with the half steps occurring between the third and fourth tones and between the seventh and first tones

Measure: the division of a staff with bar lines according to the meter

Melodic minor: a seven-pitch minor scale starting on the sixth scale degree of its parallel major. The ascending scale features a flatted third scale degree but borrows the raised sixth and seventh scale degrees from the parallel major. The descending scale is the same as natural minor.

Meter: the combination of strong and weak beats in a recurring pattern

Motive: a musical germ that is usually repeated and developed

Natural: cancels a sharp or flat

Natural minor: a seven-pitch minor scale starting on the sixth scale degree of its parallel major. Scale degrees three, six, and seven are all flatted.

Neume: a small sign used in chant that indicates the number of pitches per syllable and the ascent or descent of the melody

Octatonic scale: a scale of eight pitches that alternate by half step and whole step

Octave: pitches of the same name separated by eight letter names

Pentatonic scale: a scale consisting of five tones in an octave

Period: a musical unit consisting of two phrases. The first phrase is musically inconclusive (usually ending with a half cadence), and the second phrase offers a more conclusive end (usually a perfect authentic cadence).

Pitch: the highness or lowness of musical sound

Phrase: the basic unit of musical thought

Range: the breadth of pitches encompassed in a musical work

Recapitulation: the third and final part of the sonata, in which the musical material from the exposition returns and brings the movement to a close

Rounded binary form: a two-part form that brings back a portion of the A section at the end of the B section to "round off" the piece

Scale: a collection of five to eight pitches arranged in either ascending or descending order

Scale degree: the number assigned to each pitch of a scale, sequentially from 1 to 7

Simple interval: an interval that spans an octave or less

Simple meter: a meter whose beat subdivides into two parts

Sharp: raises a pitch one half-step

Sonata form: a three-part form that developed in the Classical period and continued through the Romantic period. Its three parts consist of an exposition, development, and recapitulation.

Staff: the five lines and four spaces used to notate pitch

Subtonic: the seventh scale degree of a scale that is a whole step lower than the tonic

Tempo: the Italian word for *time*, in music referring to the speed of the beat.

Ternary form: a three-part (ABA) form with three sections that are harmonically closed

Tessitura: the general area of pitch (high, middle, or low) where a melody tends to lie

Timbre: the distinguishing characteristic or color of a particular musical sound

Time signature: the meter of the music as represented by two numbers. The top number indicates how many beats are in each measure; the bottom number indicates which rhythmic value receives one beat.

Tonic: the first tone of any scale; in harmony, the triad built upon the first tone of a scale

Triad: a three-note chord based on stacked thirds

Whole-tone scale: a scale that divides the octave into six, equal whole steps

FURTHER READING

Music Theory

Benward, Bruce, and J. Timothy Kolosick. *Ear Training: A Technique for Listening*. 7th ed. Boston: McGraw Hill Higher Education, 2010.

Benward, Bruce, and Marilyn Nadine Saker. *Music in Theory and Practice*. 8th ed. Vols. 1 & 2. Boston: McGraw-Hill, 2009.

Burkhart, Charles. *Anthology for Musical Analysis*. 7th ed. Boston: Schirmer Cengage Learning, 2012.

Kostka, Stefan M., and Dorothy Payne. *Tonal Harmony: With an Introduction to Twentieth-century Music*. 7th ed. New York: McGraw-Hill, 2013.

Ottman, Robert W. *Elementary Harmony: Theory and Practice*. 5th ed. Upper Saddle River, NJ: Prentice Hall, 1998.

Ottman, Robert W. *Advanced Harmony: Theory and Practice*. 5th ed. Upper Saddle River, NJ: Prentice Hall, 2000.

Phillips, Joel. *The Musician's Guide to Aural Skills*. 2nd ed. Vols. 1 & 2. New York: W.W. Norton, 2011.

Music History and Music Appreciation

David, Ron. *The History of Opera For Beginners*. Danbury, CT: For Beginners, 2013.

Endris, R. Ryan. *The History of Classical Music For Beginners*. Danbury, CT: For Beginners, 2014.

Hanning, Barbara Russano. *Concise History of Western Music*. 5th ed. New York: W.W. Norton, 2014.

Kamien, Roger. *Music: An Appreciation*.11th ed. New York: McGraw-Hill Higher Education, 2014

Steinberg, Michael. *Choral Masterworks: A Listener's Guide*. New York: Oxford University Press, 2005.

Steinberg, Michael, and Larry Rothe. *For the Love of Music: Invitations to Listening*. New York: Oxford University Press, 2006.

Steinberg, Michael. *The Symphony: A Listener's Guide*. New York: Oxford University Press, 1995.

ABOUT THE AUTHOR AND ILLUSTRATOR

R. RYAN ENDRIS, D.Mus, currently serves as Assistant Professor of Music and Director of Choral Activities at Colgate University, where he teaches courses in music theory and music appreciation and conducts the university's two choral ensembles. He is also in demand as an arranger of choral and instrumental music throughout the country, and he has conducted concerts internationally in Austria, the Czech Republic, Greece, Hungary, and Slovakia. Dr. Endris holds Doctor of Music and Master of Music of Choral Conducting degrees from the Indiana University Jacobs School of Music, as well as a Bachelor of Music Education. He studied voice with internationally acclaimed soprano Sylvia McNair, and his conducting teachers and mentors include Robert Porco of the Cleveland Orchestra; Jan Harrington of Indiana University; John Poole of the BBC Singers; and Vance George, Director Emeritus of the San Francisco Symphony Chorus.

JOE LEE is an illustrator, cartoonist, writer, and clown. With a degree from Indiana University centering on Medieval History, Joe is also a graduate of Ringling Brothers, Barnum and Bailey's Clown College. He is the author and illustrator of *Greek Mythology For Beginners* and *Dante For Beginners*, as well as the illustrator of a baker's dozen of other For Beginners titles, including: *Shakespeare*, *Postmodernism*, *Deconstruction*, and *The History of Classical Music*. Joe lives in Bloomington, Indiana with his wife Mary Bess, son Brandon, cat George, and the terriers (or rather terrors) Max and Jack.

NOTES

THE FOR BEGINNERS® SERIES